Is Legalized Marijuana Good for Society?

Patricia D. Netzley

INCONTROVERSY

ReferencePoint
Press®

San Diego, CA

Foreword

In 2008, as the US economy and economies worldwide were falling into the worst recession since the Great Depression, most Americans had difficulty comprehending the complexity, magnitude, and scope of what was happening. As is often the case with a complex, controversial issue such as this historic global economic recession, looking at the problem as a whole can be overwhelming and often does not lead to understanding. One way to better comprehend such a large issue or event is to break it into smaller parts. The intricacies of global economic recession may be difficult to understand, but one can gain insight by instead beginning with an individual contributing factor, such as the real estate market. When examined through a narrower lens, complex issues become clearer and easier to evaluate.

This is the idea behind ReferencePoint Press's *In Controversy* series. The series examines the complex, controversial issues of the day by breaking them into smaller pieces. Rather than looking at the stem cell research debate as a whole, a title would examine an important aspect of the debate such as *Is Stem Cell Research Necessary?* or *Is Embryonic Stem Cell Research Ethical?* By studying the central issues of the debate individually, researchers gain a more solid and focused understanding of the topic as a whole.

Each book in the series provides a clear, insightful discussion of the issues, integrating facts and a variety of contrasting opinions for a solid, balanced perspective. Personal accounts and direct quotes from academic and professional experts, advocacy groups, politicians, and others enhance the narrative. Sidebars add depth to the discussion by expanding on important ideas and events. For quick reference, a list of key facts concludes every chapter. Source notes, an annotated organizations list, bibliography, and index provide student researchers with additional tools for papers and class discussion.

Foreword

In 2008, as the US economy and economies worldwide were falling into the worst recession since the Great Depression, most Americans had difficulty comprehending the complexity, magnitude, and scope of what was happening. As is often the case with a complex, controversial issue such as this historic global economic recession, looking at the problem as a whole can be overwhelming and often does not lead to understanding. One way to better comprehend such a large issue or event is to break it into smaller parts. The intricacies of global economic recession may be difficult to understand, but one can gain insight by instead beginning with an individual contributing factor, such as the real estate market. When examined through a narrower lens, complex issues become clearer and easier to evaluate.

This is the idea behind ReferencePoint Press's *In Controversy* series. The series examines the complex, controversial issues of the day by breaking them into smaller pieces. Rather than looking at the stem cell research debate as a whole, a title would examine an important aspect of the debate such as *Is Stem Cell Research Necessary?* or *Is Embryonic Stem Cell Research Ethical?* By studying the central issues of the debate individually, researchers gain a more solid and focused understanding of the topic as a whole.

Each book in the series provides a clear, insightful discussion of the issues, integrating facts and a variety of contrasting opinions for a solid, balanced perspective. Personal accounts and direct quotes from academic and professional experts, advocacy groups, politicians, and others enhance the narrative. Sidebars add depth to the discussion by expanding on important ideas and events. For quick reference, a list of key facts concludes every chapter. Source notes, an annotated organizations list, bibliography, and index provide student researchers with additional tools for papers and class discussion.

Contents

About the Author

Patricia D. Netzley has written more than sixty books for children, teens, and adults. She has also worked as an editor and a writing instructor and is a member of the Society of Children's Book Writers and Illustrators.

© 2015 ReferencePoint Press, Inc.
Printed in the United States

For more information, contact:
ReferencePoint Press, Inc.
PO Box 27779
San Diego, CA 92198
www.ReferencePointPress.com

LIBRARY OF CONGRESS CATALOGING-IN-PUBLICATION DATA

Netzley, Patricia D.
  Is legalized marijuana good for society? / by Patricia D. Netzley.
    pages cm. — (In controversy)
  Includes bibliographical references and index.
  ISBN-13: 978-1-60152-774-5 (hardback)
  ISBN-10: 1-60152-774-8 (hardback)
  1. Marijuana—United States—Juvenile literature. 2. Marijuana abuse—United States—Juvenile literature. 3. Drug legalization—United States—Juvenile literature. I. Title.
  HV5822.M3N47 2015
  363.4—dc23
                                                                    2014033996

Is Legalized Marijuana Good for Society?

Patricia D. Netzley

INCONTROVERSY

ReferencePoint
Press®

San Diego, CA

The *In Controversy* series also challenges students to think critically about issues, to improve their problem-solving skills, and to sharpen their ability to form educated opinions. As President Barack Obama stated in a March 2009 speech, success in the twenty-first century will not be measurable merely by students' ability to "fill in a bubble on a test but whether they possess 21st century skills like problem-solving and critical thinking and entrepreneurship and creativity." Those who possess these skills will have a strong foundation for whatever lies ahead.

No one can know for certain what sort of world awaits today's students. What we can assume, however, is that those who are inquisitive about a wide range of issues; open-minded to divergent views; aware of bias and opinion; and able to reason, reflect, and reconsider will be best prepared for the future. As the international development organization Oxfam notes, "Today's young people will grow up to be the citizens of the future: but what that future holds for them is uncertain. We can be quite confident, however, that they will be faced with decisions about a wide range of issues on which people have differing, contradictory views. If they are to develop as global citizens all young people should have the opportunity to engage with these controversial issues."

In Controversy helps today's students better prepare for tomorrow. An understanding of the complex issues that drive our world and the ability to think critically about them are essential components of contributing, competing, and succeeding in the twenty-first century.

Harmful or Beneficial?

I n July 2014 the *New York Times* published an editorial calling on the US government to end the bans on growing, selling, possessing, and using marijuana (also known as cannabis), a drug derived from a flowering plant with properties that can affect mood and behavior as well as human health. The editorial compared marijuana criminalization to Prohibition, a period from 1920 to 1933 when alcohol was similarly banned, saying: "It took 13 years for the United States to come to its senses and end Prohibition, 13 years in which people kept drinking, otherwise law-abiding citizens became criminals and crime syndicates arose and flourished. It has been more than 40 years since Congress passed the current ban on marijuana, inflicting great harm on society just to prohibit a substance far less dangerous than alcohol."[1]

This harm, the *Times* argues, stems from the fact that many otherwise law-abiding citizens use marijuana, whether because of its health benefits or because they like the way it makes them feel, and the resulting arrests for illegally possessing and/or ingesting the substance can ruin these people's lives. The newspaper reports that in 2012, according to the Federal Bureau of Investigation (FBI), there were 658,000 arrests for marijuana possession. Moreover, the majority of these arrests affected black men, which suggests to the *Times* that there is a racist component to the enforcement of marijuana laws—yet another reason, the editorial says, to end the prohibition of marijuana.

Public Support

The publication of the *Times* editorial reignited a long-standing debate over whether banning marijuana is good for society. But responses to the editorial showed what polls have already found: that a majority of Americans—58 percent, according to an October 2013 poll by the Gallup organization—support legalizing marijuana for adults age twenty-one and older. The *Times* informal poll of its readers suggests that this number might be far higher; within roughly two days after the publication of the editorial, the newspaper had received 4,043 votes in favor of legalization as compared to 206 against and 41 unsure.

In summarizing the comments, the *Times* says that many of its readers believe that the government should not be wasting money enforcing a ban on what to many is a harmless activity. One reader, Rusty Shackleford of Indiana, writes in part, "It is the biggest waste of federal money you can imagine. . . . Alcohol and tobacco are far more dangerous and both are highly addictive substances. Marijuana is not."[2]

"It has been more than 40 years since Congress passed the current ban on marijuana, inflicting great harm on society just to prohibit a substance far less dangerous than alcohol."[1]

— *New York Times* editorial board.

Is It Harmless?

But in a response to the editorial on its website for the Office of National Drug Control Policy (ONDCP), the White House counters that marijuana is far from harmless: "In its argument, the *New York Times* editorial team failed to mention a cascade of public health problems associated with the increased availability of marijuana. While law enforcement will always play an important role in combating violent crime associated with the drug trade, the Obama Administration approaches substance use as a public health issue, not merely a criminal justice problem."[3]

The federal government's position is that marijuana is a highly addictive drug and that the consequences of this addiction can be extremely damaging to society. But according to the National Institute on Drug Abuse (NIDA), while marijuana can be addictive, the risk of becoming addicted is relatively low. In fact, experts report that the addiction potential for marijuana is far less than for caffeine, tobacco, alcohol, cocaine, or heroin.

Health Benefits

But even if the risk of addiction were higher, some people say, they would still use marijuana because of its health benefits. The marijuana plant contains over four hundred chemicals with painkilling, antibiotic, and anti-inflammatory properties. Studies suggest that burning the plant and inhaling the resulting smoke bestows these benefits as well. Studies have also shown that marijuana can stimulate appetite in people with illnesses that make them uninterested in food, alleviate the nausea and vomiting experienced by cancer patients undergoing chemotherapy, and be helpful in treating glaucoma (an eye condition) and some seizure disorders. In addition, some users have reported that marijuana has eased their depression, anxiety, insomnia, and chronic pain issues.

For recreational users the attraction of marijuana is its positive affect on mood because it can cause relaxation and/or euphoria. However, marijuana can also cause feelings of detachment, anxiety, and paranoia; and some studies suggest it can reduce motivation

or, if use is begun at a young age, even lower IQ. Many experts say, however, that the effects associated with using the drug depend on the individual, the way the marijuana is ingested, and the strength of the chemicals within any particular batch of the substance.

Most marijuana used today comes from one of two species of the plant, *Cannabis sativa* or *Cannabis indica*. In either case it is perhaps most commonly ingested in the form of dried, shredded flowers and leaves that can be smoked like tobacco in a cigarette or pipe. It can also be brewed in a tea, heated and inhaled through a vaporizer, or consumed in the form of a butter or oil used in cooking or baking or as a powder that can be taken in pill capsules.

But regardless of the method of ingestion, experts say that the potency of THC (tetrahydracannabinol), the chemical that gives marijuana its intoxicating effects, is far higher today than thirty years ago due to changes in growing practices. Specifically, the THC in marijuana averaged nearly 15 percent in 2012 as compared to around 4 percent in the 1980s. People opposed to legalizing marijuana argue that this increased potency, and the fact that potency varies by batch, make the substance too dangerous to use.

But some people argue that whether the drug is harmful is a separate issue from whether it should be legalized. These people believe that adults should have the right to use whatever substance they want—whether it be marijuana, alcohol, tobacco, or something else—without government interference. For example, one reader wrote to the *Times*: "I reject the Federal Government's right to decide what I put in my body. Even if it was 'bad' for you, so what? We don't ban skydiving, driving in cars, . . . sugary foods and beverages, . . . caffeine, ibuprofen, alcohol, cigarettes or prescription drugs, all of which are statistically more likely to harm you."[4]

Others counter that people who do not want to be exposed to marijuana have rights, too. They will have to deal with users' smoke, for example, and the possibility that their children might get their hands on marijuana. John Hawkins, a columnist with Townhall.com, suggests that legalizing marijuana would damage American society and says, "Would you want to live in a neighborhood filled with people who regularly smoke marijuana? Would you want your kids regularly smoking pot?"[5]

Hawkins also questions why people would want to make yet another vice legal, saying: "We all recognize that smoking is a dirty habit that makes you die younger while drinking is a potentially dangerous habit that leads to hundreds of thousands of deaths per year, but we want to condone pot use on top of that? That's like saying you've got a bad back and a bad shoulder; so why not break your knee cap to top it all off."[6]

Despite such arguments, as of August 1, 2014, twenty-three states and the District of Columbia have legalized marijuana for medical purposes, which means that adult residents of those states who have a prescription for the drug from a licensed physician can purchase and use marijuana. Colorado and Washington have legalized marijuana for recreational use as well. Their recreational marijuana laws went into effect in 2014, too recently to tell how they will impact society. Nor are there any models abroad to indicate what this impact might be. Although several countries consider marijuana possession to be a minor offense rather than a criminal one, only one country, Uruguay, has legalized the production, sale, and consumption of marijuana. However, Uruguay's president Jose Mujica has postponed the law's implementation until 2015.

Without a clear idea of how to handle legalization, the federal government has vacillated on whether to challenge the right of states to enact such laws. The US Department of Justice (DOJ) announced in August 2013 that it will not interfere with state sales of marijuana unless it determines that marijuana legalization is causing serious harm to individuals and society—and yet federal authorities continue to arrest anyone they find in possession of marijuana, even in places where marijuana is legal under state law. Consequently, much confusion surrounds the issue of whether using marijuana is acceptable, and people continue to disagree on the harmfulness of the substance.

"Would you want to live in a neighborhood filled with people who regularly smoke marijuana? Would you want your kids regularly smoking pot?"[5]

— John Hawkins, a columnist with Townhall.com.

Facts

- Based on reports from defectors from North Korea, experts believe that this secretive country either has legalized marijuana or does not enforce its laws against marijuana.

- Estimates of the number of marijuana users in the United States vary widely, but according to the Substance Abuse and Mental Health Services Administration (SAMHSA) about 12 percent of Americans over the age of twelve have used marijuana within the past year.

- According to NIDA, the number of high school students who use marijuana has been on the rise since the 1990s, and if this trend continues marijuana smoking will soon become more popular among young people than cigarette smoking.

- The United Nations reports that over 158 million people around the world use marijuana.

- According to the American Civil Liberties Union (ACLU), black people are 3.7 times more likely to be arrested for marijuana possession than whites even though blacks and whites use marijuana at roughly the same rates.

- The ACLU reports that in some US counties, blacks are thirty times more likely to be arrested for marijuana possession than whites.

What Are the Origins of the Marijuana Legalization Controversy?

To understand today's arguments surrounding the issue of whether people should be allowed to use marijuana, it is necessary to examine the decision to ban the drug in the first place. This occurred during the 1930s, when people gave more thought to how marijuana impacts human behavior than to what the evidence related to its effects on human health might be. Specifically, beginning in the 1920s people became concerned that marijuana use went hand in hand with criminal and deviant behavior, and prejudices against users drove many of the discussions related to criminalization.

Cures for Ills

Americans' first association with cannabis plants was in the form of hemp, a member of the species that has a negligible amount of THC and therefore does not have the mood-altering effects of marijuana. Its fiber can be used to manufacture items such as rope, clothing, and sails, making it so important during Colonial times that people were legally required to grow it. As the country expanded, hemp-growing became an industry that provided many useful products.

In the 1840s Americans also discovered, largely thanks to the work of physician William Brooke O'Shaughnessy in Ireland, that other members of the cannabis family had curative properties. This information had already been known for centuries in non-Western parts of the world. O'Shaughnessy conducted scientific studies that found the plant could be used as a drug to treat such health problems as asthma, migraines, insomnia, menstrual difficulties, anxiety, lack of appetite, and convulsions. By the latter part of the nineteenth century American physicians were prescribing cannabis for a variety of ills.

The most typical form of the drug at that time was tincture of cannabis. It was and still is made by mixing cannabis flowers and trimmed leaves with alcohol in order to extract the plant's cannabinoids, the active compounds in cannabis. Using a dropper, the resulting liquid is placed under a patient's tongue and then absorbed into the body.

Fraudulent Products

During the same period cannabis was a common though often secret ingredient in elixirs sold either by traveling salesmen or over the counter in stores. There were hundreds of such concoctions, many of them patent medicines—medicines that were advertised as being effective cures when in fact they were either worthless or harmful. In 1905 investigative journalist Samuel Hopkins Adams published a series of articles exposing these frauds, which led to the passage the following year of the Pure Food and Drug Act.

A federal consumer protection law, the Pure Food and Drug Act included the requirement that medicines be accurately labeled to show whether they contained certain drugs and if so, in what amount. These drugs included not only cannabis but also alcohol, cocaine, heroin, and morphine, all of which the law recognized as being habit-forming. But in many states the drugs were still allowed to be sold over the counter without a prescription. Other states, however, passed laws requiring that the drugs be sold by prescription only, concerned that their sale needed to be controlled due to their addictive properties.

Hemp fibers have long been used to make rope (pictured), clothing, and sails. Although hemp comes from the same plant as marijuana, it does not have the same mood-altering effects as the drug.

The Spread of Recreational Use

Shortly after the federal government mandated the disclosure of the use of cannabis in medicinal elixirs, Americans began using the substance recreationally for changing their mood—today called "getting high" or "getting stoned." Some historians believe the practice first entered the United States in approximately 1900 via Texas border towns, brought there by Mexican immigrants who called the substance they smoked *marihuana*—a name that soon replaced *cannabis* as the most common way to refer to the drug. Others believe Mexican immigrants brought this substance into the country, all along the US-Mexico border, in around 1910. In either case, by 1915 Texas grocery stores and drugstores were selling *marihuana* throughout the country via mail order, typically labeling it a Mexican herb.

Also during this period sailors and West Indian immigrants brought the substance to the port city of New Orleans, Louisiana. There the popularity of smoking marijuana grew among the black jazz musicians who played in bordellos and other places of ill repute. As these musicians spread their form of music, which was then new, into the Midwest and East, they spread recreational marijuana use as well.

Association with Minorities

Given marijuana's connection to black jazz musicians and Mexican immigrants, in the early twentieth century white Americans strongly associated marijuana use with minorities. Consequently, when politicians and others wanted to stir up racism against a particular minority group, they often did so by demonizing marijuana use. For example, those opposed to allowing Mexican immigrants into the country—largely on the grounds that the immigrants were taking jobs away from American citizens—claimed that using the drug led to insanity and violent crime, and they dubbed marijuana *loco weed*. (*Loco* is the Spanish word for *crazy*).

During a debate in Texas on whether marijuana should be banned there, one senator said: "All Mexicans are crazy and this stuff [marijuana] is what makes them crazy."[7] In Montana, a legislator stated: "When some beet field peon takes a few traces of this stuff . . . he thinks he has just been elected president of Mexico, so he starts out to execute all his political enemies."[8]

Similarly, a 1934 newspaper editorial accused the drug of making black men forget their place, which at the time was to be subservient to whites. The editorial states: "Marihuana influences Negroes to look at white people in the eye, step on white men's shadows and look at a white woman twice."[9]

Stirring Fears

In Northern California, Henry J. Finger, a member of the California Board of Pharmacy, not only attacked a minority group for its cannabis use but also suggested that whites were being corrupted by it. Specifically, he complained about an influx of immigrants from East India by saying: "Within the last year we in California have been getting a large influx of Hindoos and they have in turn started quite a demand for cannabis indica; they are a very undesirable lot and the habit is growing in California very fast . . . the fear is now that they are initiating our whites into this habit."[10] (Though Finger called the immigrants "Hindoos," these people practiced the Sikh religion, not Hinduism.)

In other places newspaper articles claimed that marijuana users were accosting children outside of schools in order to convince them to use the drug. There were also stories of robberies being committed by bands of marijuana users, and law enforcement officers claimed that murderers smoked marijuana prior to their crime in order to reach the frenzy necessary to commit it.

A 1905 *Los Angeles Times* article included a report typical of this era: "Not long ago a man who had smoked a marihuana cigarette attacked and killed a policeman and badly wounded three others; six policemen were needed to disarm him and march him to the police station where he had to be put into a straight jacket. Such occurrences are frequent."[11]

Similarly, in El Paso, Texas, Chief Deputy Stanley Good reported in 1915: "The most atrocious crimes which have come under the notice of the local police and sheriff's departments have been attributed to marijuana fiends. One under its influence is devoid of fear and as reckless of consequences or results. There are instances where the drug crazed victim has been placed in jail, but in many cases officers have been compelled to slay the fiend in order to save their own lives."[12]

Harry Anslinger

As a result of Good's insistence that marijuana users were to be feared, the city of El Paso banned the drug in 1915. But this was not the first such ban. Fears about marijuana users convinced the voters of California to pass the earliest such law in 1913, which banned all products containing hemp or loco weed throughout the state. (The text of the law specifically used the term *loco weed* for marijuana.) Other states soon followed suit, and by 1930 marijuana was illegal in thirty states.

But for one man, this state-by-state criminalization of marijuana was not enough. Harry Anslinger, the first commissioner of

Reefer Madness

In 1936 a church group financed the production of a film entitled *Tell Your Children* to warn parents about the horrible things that would happen to young people who tried marijuana. In the film the drug leads various high school students to commit attempted rape, murder, and suicide; and in the end their drug dealer is committed to an insane asylum. Shortly after *Tell Your Children* was created, it was bought by producer Dwain Esper, who reedited and distributed it throughout the country from 1938 through the 1950s under various titles, the most famous of which is *Reefer Madness*. At this point it was considered an exploitation film, a low-budget movie designed to exploit an interest in lurid subject matter, and most viewers took this subject matter seriously. But in the 1970s the film was rediscovered by people fighting for marijuana legalization who considered it a satire. Since then, the phrase *reefer madness* has generally come to refer to a severe craving that arises after going for a while without smoking marijuana.

the US Bureau of Narcotics—created in 1930 to consolidate efforts related to narcotic drugs under one federal agency—wanted to end marijuana use throughout the United States. Before becoming the nation's first so-called drug czar, Anslinger was an enforcement agent for Prohibition, and he was disappointed that this nationwide constitutional ban on alcohol had failed to end alcohol consumption in the United States. He believed that its failure could in part be blamed on the fact that the public did not understand just how harmful the substance was.

Determined to make sure people recognized how dangerous marijuana was, Anslinger made many statements demonizing the drug and its users, particularly minorities. In fact, he said that "the primary reason to outlaw marijuana is its effect on the degenerate races."[13] He also insisted that the drug could turn young people

into killers, and on at least one occasion he related an incident of
horrific brutality to prove his point:

> An entire family was murdered by a youthful (marijuana)
> addict in Florida. When the officers arrived at the home
> they found the youth staggering about in a human slaugh-
> terhouse. With an axe he had killed his father, mother, two
> brothers and a sister. He seemed to be in a daze . . . he had
> no recollection of having committed the multiple crime.

The officers knew him ordinarily as a sane, rather quiet young man; now he was pitifully crazed. They sought the reason. The boy said he had been in the habit of smoking something which youthful friends called "muggles," a childish name for marijuana.[14]

This story was repeated in numerous articles between 1935 and 1937, despite the fact that there is no proof the incident actually occurred. In fact, many historians believe that Anslinger made it up. Nonetheless, it and similar tales did much to convince the public that marijuana truly was dangerous.

The Marihuana Tax Act of 1937

Anslinger also wanted to restrict access to marijuana. But rather than call for the substance to be made illegal nationwide—an approach that had proved so unsuccessful during Prohibition—he drafted a bill that would impose a one-dollar tax on anyone who bought, sold, imported, or grew marijuana, cannabis, or hemp commercially and/or possessed it and/or prescribed the substance, with the prescribers including not just physicians but veterinarians. The penalties for not paying this tax would be a fine of up to $2,000 and five years' imprisonment.

The bill also laid out how the tax would be collected, but Anslinger did not provide access to its full text until shortly before Congress considered its passage. As a result the American Medical Association (AMA), which objected to any such tax because of its effect on physicians, did not have time to present a proper argument against it. This lack of argument, along with Anslinger's impassioned testimony during congressional hearings into the bill, led to a quick passage of the Marihuana Tax Act of 1937.

Shortly thereafter readers of the new law discovered that it included many requirements that would make it difficult for physicians to pay the one-dollar tax. Specifically, to prescribe marijuana for a patient, a physician had to purchase a one-dollar tax stamp, but this could not be done without immediately and officially reporting to the Federal Bureau of Narcotics, under oath, the patient's name and address, the reason the drug was necessary, the dates it would be prescribed, the doses used, and other pertinent information. If this was not done, then not only the physician but the patient would also be at risk of being fined and imprisoned. Facing this possibility, many physicians stopped prescribing marijuana.

Federal Arrests Begin

The Tax Act also granted the commissioner of the Bureau of Narcotics—Anslinger—and his agents with the Treasury Department the authority to enforce the law as police would. This made it easy for Anslinger to ensure that the public would realize the serious consequences of disobeying his new law. He ordered his agents to make several high-profile arrests of people who failed to pay the tax, with the first arrest occurring the day the act was enacted into law.

Specifically, on October 2, 1937, FBI agents and local police raided a hotel in Denver, Colorado, where fifty-eight-year-old farmer Samuel R. Caldwell was in the process of handing two or three marijuana cigarettes to twenty-six-year-old Moses Baca as part of a trade. When Caldwell later went before a judge for his crime, he was shown no mercy. Judge Foster Symes told him: "I consider marijuana the worst of all narcotics, far worse than the use of morphine or cocaine. Under its influence men become beasts. Marijuana destroys life itself. I have no sympathy with those who sell this weed. The government is going to enforce this new law to the letter."[15] Caldwell was sentenced to four years of hard labor in a federal penitentiary and fined $1,000. He served every day of this sentence, and Baca served every day of an eighteen-month prison sentence.

> "I consider marijuana the worst of all narcotics, far worse than the use of morphine or cocaine. Under its influence men become beasts."[15]
>
> — US District Court Judge Foster Symes.

Even Tougher Sentences

Now that the act was law, Anslinger decided to curtail the spread of stories that made it sound like marijuana created crazed killers. In April 1938 he advised his agents: "Our present policy is to discourage undue emphasis on marihuana for the reason that in some sections of the country recently press reports have been so exaggerated that interest in the subject has become almost hysterical and we are therefore trying to mold public opinion along more conservative and saner lines."[16] He also began an education campaign to encourage federal judges to get tough on offenders.

The US Supreme Court Weighs In

In August 2002 officers from the Butte County, California, sheriff's department and agents from the DEA seized and destroyed six marijuana plants belonging to Diane Monson. Monson had been using the marijuana to relieve pain and muscle spasms in her back that were due to a car accident. She was also providing marijuana to Angel Raich, who also suffered from severe pain. Raich had tried other pain relievers and discovered she was allergic to them. After their plants were seized, Raich and Monson both sued the federal government, arguing that they were entitled to use marijuana under state law and that the federal Controlled Substances Act that denied them their right to use marijuana was unconstitutional. Eventually their case reached the US Supreme Court, which in June 2005 held that Congress has the right to ban people from growing or using marijuana, and this ban can be enforced even in states that have decreed marijuana is legal.

At the same time, he directed his agency to concentrate on major cases, leaving the smaller ones for local jurisdictions to handle. During the 1940s even significant cases were being handled at the state level because the bureau was putting most of its attention on addressing a growing problem with another category of drugs: opiates, which are powerful narcotics such as opium, codeine, and morphine.

Then in the late 1940s the public began to express concerns about young people using marijuana, and some said that marijuana might be a stepping-stone to using harder drugs, particularly heroin. As a result, Congress held hearings on the issue and, unlike the 1937 hearings, these included testimony from a respected expert on marijuana's physical, psychological, and behavioral effects on humans. Harris Isbell, director of research at the Public Health Service Hospital in Lexington, Kentucky, testified that the drug's use did not lead to insanity or increased violence and reported that "smoking marijuana has no unpleasant aftereffects, no dependence is developed on the drug, and the practice can easily be stopped at any time."[17]

Nonetheless, Congress toughened penalties related to marijuana possession and selling, and it did this again in 1956. Both times the Bureau of Narcotics called on states to make their penalties match those at the federal level, and many complied. This often resulted in severer penalties for possessing marijuana than for more serious crimes. For example, from 1958 to 1969 in the Commonwealth of Virginia, the punishment for possessing marijuana or any other illegal drug was a mandatory minimum sentence in prison of twenty years with no eligibility to reduce that time. In contrast, the punishment for first-degree murder was a mandatory minimum sentence of fifteen years.

"Smoking marijuana has no unpleasant aftereffects, no dependence is developed on the drug, and the practice can easily be stopped at any time."[17]

— Harris Isbell, director of research at the Public Health Service Hospital in Lexington, Kentucky, in 1951.

The War on Drugs

However, harsh sentences did little to deter young people from trying marijuana, and during the 1960s the public became uncomfortable seeing students receive years in prison for what was increasingly viewed as a relatively harmless crime. An October 1969 article in a popular magazine, *Life*, reported that 12 million people had tried marijuana, and it called a then recent case of a twenty-year-old college student, who was sentenced to twenty years for possession, a travesty. In response to the outcry over this case, President Richard Nixon called for first-time offenses to be considered misdemeanors, which would mean that sentences for such crimes would be light.

Nonetheless, in 1971 Nixon announced that he was declaring a war on drugs, and the following year he rejected the finding of the National Commission on Marihuana and Drug Abuse that drug use was private behavior and should therefore not be criminalized. In addition, his administration established the Drug Enforcement Administration (DEA) in the DOJ to combat illegal drug use and smuggling and control scientific and medical research into drug-related issues. The DEA was also responsible for the classification system that made marijuana a Schedule I drug.

This system uses two criteria—a drug's medical use and its potential to lead to addiction—to determine how the drug should be regulated. But such information was unknown in regard to marijuana when it was deemed a Schedule I controlled substance, the category reserved for drugs that are highly addictive yet offer little or no medical benefits. Consequently Roger Egeberg, Nixon's assistant secretary of health, suggested in August 1970 that marijuana's Schedule I designation might be temporary. He explained: "Since there is still a considerable void in our knowledge of the plant and effects of the active drug contained in it, our recommendation is that marijuana be retained within Schedule I at least until the completion of certain studies now underway to resolve the issue."[18]

A Lighter Approach

Most of these studies were never completed, so the issue was never resolved to the federal government's satisfaction. Nonetheless, during the 1970s many states reduced penalties for possessing marijuana. For example, in 1973 Oregon became the first state to decriminalize the possession of small amounts of cannabis. (Decriminalizing a substance does not make it legal to possess; however, it makes possessing it for personal use a civil rather than a criminal offense. This means that an offender suffers only the confiscation of the substance and a small fine.) In 1976 California changed a law making it a felony to possess small amounts of marijuana for personal use to a misdemeanor crime.

States also began passing laws allowing the possession, though not the growing or selling, of marijuana for medicinal purposes. Many of these changes in drug laws were due to efforts of groups like the National Organization for the Reform of Marijuana Laws (NORML), established in 1970 to work for the decriminalization of cannabis. In addition, the American public gradually rejected the demonization of marijuana that had been established in the 1920s and 1930s, aided in large part by the fact that not only minorities but also whites were using the substance in greater numbers.

Still, it was not until the 1990s that the first law to allow the growing and possessing of medical marijuana was passed. This legislation was enacted in California in November 1996, and two years later Oregon and Washington enacted similar laws. Since

then twenty-three states have legalized medical marijuana, with New York the most recent as of July 2014, and many more are expected to follow suit. Meanwhile the federal government has decided to take a wait-and-see attitude before considering challenging these laws, which run contrary to federal law.

Some experts say that had the controversy surrounding marijuana begun more rationally, without racist remarks and wild stories about marijuana-crazed murderers, the federal government might not now be so entrenched in maintaining the position that marijuana is among the most dangerous, harmful drugs in existence. Many criticize the US government for what the *New York Times* calls its "irrational enforcement" of laws and its determination to "[cling] to a policy that has its origins in racism and xenophobia and whose principal effect has been to ruin the lives of generations of people."[19]

The controversy surrounding the abandonment of this policy in order to nationally legalize marijuana therefore has its origin in the rationale that made it illegal. As Jon Kennedy of NORML says, "People are ready to have the discussion, 'Why is marijuana illegal in the first place?'"[20] Nonetheless, opponents to legalization say that the fact that the process that led to criminalization was flawed is a separate issue from whether the drug will damage society if it is legalized today.

FACTS

- Almost all state and federal laws related to marijuana still use the earliest spelling of the word: *marihuana*.

- There are several theories regarding the origin of the word *marihuana*, including that it comes from the Spanish girl's names Maria and Juana or is derived from a Spanish colloquialism for the "Chinese oregano"— *mejorana*—used by Chinese immigrants in western Mexico.

- Experts estimate that 2 to 5 percent of Americans were drug addicts in 1900, far more than today.

- Canada made using marijuana illegal in 1923, fourteen years before the United States criminalized the substance.

- Even though hemp contains negligible amounts of THC, in 1970 the United States banned people from growing it without a federal permit.

- The concentration of THC in marijuana today is around 12 percent, an amount four times greater than it typically was in the 1980s.

CHAPTER TWO

Do People with Illnesses Benefit from Marijuana?

Human health is the focus of many of today's discussions regarding whether the US government should pass a law making marijuana legal throughout the country. Experts report that there are currently 4.2 million medical cannabis patients in the United States, and these individuals believe they are receiving genuine medical benefits from using marijuana. But others say that even if this is the case, marijuana also has the ability to harm people and should therefore not be legal to use.

The Federal Position

The federal government maintains that marijuana is always unsafe to use and is also unproved as a medical treatment. The US Food and Drug Administration (FDA) has stated: "Marijuana has a high potential for abuse, has no currently accepted medical use in treatment in the United States, and has a lack of accepted safety for use under medical supervision."[21] Moreover, the DEA has deemed marijuana to be worthy of its Schedule I designation, and in 2012 the department's chief, Michele M. Leonhart, declared that it and all other illegal drugs are bad.

The government's position has adversely affected research into whether marijuana actually does have health benefits. Under federal law NIDA and the DEA must approve all marijuana research, and researchers can use only marijuana provided by the federal government. The process to acquire this marijuana is long and fraught with red tape.

Moreover, because marijuana is a Schedule I drug, federal authorities are reluctant to authorize studying its health effects on human subjects. Therefore most of the studies into marijuana's health benefits take place in other countries, including Israel and the United Kingdom (UK). In fact, only 6 percent of research into marijuana in the United States is related to studying its medical properties.

Thwarted Research

As an example of how the federal government can adversely affect research into marijuana's health benefits, for over ten years it has repeatedly rejected an application to establish a farm as part of the Medicinal Plant Program at the University of Massachusetts Amherst that would grow marijuana for medical researchers. The program's director, horticulturist Lyle Craker, reports that this situation will not change even if Massachusetts legalizes marijuana, because growing and using the substance will still be illegal at the federal level. In fact, he says that despite the fact that many other states have legalized marijuana, "any real research is still restricted."[22]

"Marijuana has a high potential for abuse, has no currently accepted medical use in treatment in the United States, and has a lack of accepted safety for use under medical supervision."[21]

—US Food and Drug Administration.

Another example of thwarted American research is an eleven-year project in California that was put on hold in 2012 because of a lack of support. This state-funded project involved clinical studies of medical marijuana through the Center for Medical Cannabis Research at the University of California at San Diego. When California legislators cut off the project's funding because of budget problems, the center was unable to turn to the federal government for financial help. Moreover, without the state to help project leaders navigate the federal red tape, according to center director Igor Grant, even if funds were found elsewhere it would be difficult to conduct the study. He says, "I think an ordinary researcher without the support of the state would be hard pressed to do it. It's just a difficult and cumbersome process."[23]

Easing Pain

That the center's project has been suspended is unfortunate because its human clinical trials found that cannabis is effective in

treating pain and spasticity (stiff and rigid muscles) in people suffering from multiple sclerosis and HIV. Experts believe that the reason for this relief is the THC found in the plant. Researchers have learned that this chemical binds with receptors in muscles, nerves, and the brain to reduce pain.

Sometimes the lessening of pain can be dramatic. This was the case, for example, with a sufferer of rheumatoid arthritis (RA)—a progressive disease that causes inflammation in joints—who received permission from the state of Rhode Island in 2006 to grow his own marijuana for medical purposes. He reports: "If my pain is at a 10, it will take it down to a 6 or 6.5."[24] In addition, studies with RA sufferers have found that THC reduces their pain and joint inflammation enough to improve their sleep.

Inflammatory Bowel Diseases

Marijuana's ability to reduce inflammation has proved helpful in treating inflammatory bowel diseases as well. The substance also decreases emesis (vomiting), gastric acid secretion, and intestinal motility (the movement of food content during the process of digestion) in sufferers of these diseases. A 2010 study at the University of Nottingham in the UK found that THC and cannabidiol (CBD), another chemical in marijuana that also appears to have medicinal properties, make it more difficult for bacteria to penetrate the walls of the intestine.

A 2013 study at the Meir Medical Center in Israel suggests that marijuana might also trigger a complete remission in an inflammatory bowel disease known as Crohn's disease. The patients in this study had a severe form of the disease, and no other therapies had provided them with relief. After eight weeks, of the eleven patients who smoked a cannabis cigarette twice a day as opposed to ten patients who smoked a placebo cigarette, five no longer had the pain, nausea, fatigue, and weight loss that were symptomatic of their disease. Five more experienced a marked reduction in these symptoms. In addition, all of the patients in the cannabis group reported that their appetite and sleep had improved.

"If my pain is at a 10, [marijuana] will take it down to a 6 or 6.5." [24]

— A rheumatoid arthritis patient in Rhode Island.

Glaucoma

Another beneficial quality of marijuana is its ability to reduce pressure in the eye. This makes it an effective treatment for glaucoma, a group of progressive eye diseases that increase eye pressure. The excess pressure causes cells in the eye to die and nerve fibers to degenerate, damaging the optic nerve, and any vision lost during this process will not be recovered. If left untreated—or if not caught early enough—the disease can cause blindness; and standard treatments including eye drops, pills, and surgery have varying degrees of success.

Marijuana's effectiveness in fighting glaucoma was discovered in the 1970s, and in 1976 this treatment led to a landmark legal decision. The focus of the case was Robert C. Randall, a twenty-eight-year-old man with glaucoma whose doctor had previously told him he would be blind before he reached the age of thirty regardless of which conventional treatments were used. This news led Randall to try marijuana, and when he discovered that it improved his eyesight

Medication for Football Players

In January 2014 National Football League (NFL) commissioner Roger Goodell said that the NFL might rescind its ban on using marijuana because of the substance's potential ability to help with pain and injuries. This ban is stated in the collective bargaining agreement between players and the league. By the time Goodell made this statement, several people had already suggested that NFL players be allowed to use marijuana, especially after experiencing head trauma. For example, in December 2013 Howard Bryant of the sports network ESPN said: "[The NFL] is a league in which the locker room culture still demands that athletes play through [the pain]. And given that marijuana is a legitimate pain reliever—especially for the migraines that can be a byproduct of head trauma—and is far less dangerous and potentially addictive than, say, [the narcotic pain reliever] OxyContin, it is almost immoral to deny players the right to use it." However, if the NFL were to allow players to use medical marijuana, this use could occur only in states where possession of the substance is legal.

Douglas A. Berman, "NFL Commissioner Open to Medical Marijuana as the 2014 Pot Playoffs Continue," *Marijuana Law, Policy, and Reform*, Law Professor Blogs Network, January 14, 2014. http://lawprofessors.typepad.com.

he started growing and using the substance. But in 1975 police raided his apartment and arrested him for possessing marijuana, leading Randall to sue the federal government for denying him access to a vital medicine. In preparation for this case, Randall underwent a series of tests that proved no other treatment would halt the destruction to his eyesight.

A federal district court sided with Randall, ruling that his marijuana was a medical necessity. But because it could not sanction the illegal growing of the plant in a private home, the court ordered the FDA to set up a program to provide Randall with his marijuana. This made Randall the first US citizen to be prescribed marijuana for a medical condition since marijuana's criminalization, as well as the first American to be legally entitled to marijuana grown by the government.

Protecting the Brain

Marijuana also appears to be better than other drugs in treating Alzheimer's disease, which causes mental deterioration. In 2006 scientists at the Scripps Research Institute reported in the journal *Molecular Pharmaceutics* that THC inhibits the formation of amyloid plaque, one of two brain abnormalities that occur in Alzheimer's patients, and appears to be a more successful weapon against the disease than any of the drugs then approved to treat it. Moreover, THC is effective in fighting not only the symptoms of the disease but its progression too. This is particularly important because, according to the Alzheimer's Association, the disease is the sixth-leading cause of death in the country.

Other studies have shown that marijuana can protect the brain from damage subsequent to a stroke, a concussion, or a trauma. Research with rodents has shown that after a brain injury of this nature, cannabis can lessen or prevent bruising, promote healing, improve brain function, and/or shrink damaged areas of the brain. However, Dale Webb, director of research and information at the Stroke Association in the UK, cautions: "Further research is needed to investigate whether cannabinoids have the same effects in humans: the effects of cannabis on the brain are highly complex and it remains a risky substance."[25]

"Further research is needed to investigate whether cannabinoids have the same [positive] effects in humans [as in rats]: the effects of cannabis on the brain are highly complex and it remains a risky substance."[25]

— Dale Webb, director of research and information at the British Stroke Association.

Spasms, Tremors, and Seizures

However, rat studies led to the discovery in 2003 at Virginia Commonwealth University that marijuana reduces epileptic seizures. After receiving either a marijuana extract or synthetic marijuana, the rats were seizure-free for ten hours. Experts theorize that this is because one or more of the chemicals in marijuana bind to brain cells in the area of the brain responsible for triggering seizures.

In any case, marijuana is now being used to treat Dravet syndrome, a rare and severe form of epilepsy that begins in infancy. Physicians use a strain of marijuana that is high in CBD and low in THC to decrease patients' symptoms. This combination calms the part of the brain that brings on seizures, thereby reducing their number.

As an example of how successful this approach can be, five-year-old Charlotte Figi's seizures dropped from roughly three hundred a week—despite the fact that she was on seven different medications for her disorder—to just two or three a month after she started treatment. These results were so remarkable that neurosurgeon Sanjay Gupta, a respected expert on health-related issues, included the case in his documentary on marijuana, *Weed*. He also said that it was influential in convincing him that marijuana should be legalized.

Gupta's documentary also presented the case of a sufferer of Leeuwenhoek's disease, which causes the muscles of the abdomen to spasm. The man's physicians had failed to find a prescription medicine that would successfully treat his condition. But using marijuana as soon as an attack begins quickly eases the spasms. Similarly, in 2013 researchers at Tel Aviv University in Israel found that smoking marijuana eases the tremors and muscle rigidity of Parkinson's disease.

Nausea

Among the most widely recognized benefits of marijuana is its ability to end nausea. The drug is often used to lessen the debilitating pain and nausea that accompany chemotherapy treatments for cancer, and it can stimulate the appetites of cancer patients as well. In addition, marijuana can lessen nausea in patients being treated for hepatitis C, a blood disease, and those suffering from lupus, an autoimmune disorder. In fact, marijuana is so effective at relieving nausea, whatever its cause, that the FDA recognizes the drug's value in this regard.

However, for the FDA to consider a substance to be a legitimate medicine, every dose must have the same number and potency of ingredients, which is not the case with marijuana. The chemical compounds in each plant are not consistent from one

plant to the next, and the way the plant matter is prepared for smoking can also affect potency. Moreover, the process of smoking makes it difficult to gauge just how much of the chemicals the smoker is inhaling. The FDA cannot approve marijuana as a nausea medicine because of these factors.

Nevertheless, the FDA has approved drugs that contain synthetic versions or similar versions of the chemicals found in marijuana. These are typically in pill form and available by prescription. In addition, a relatively new medicine called Sativex, which contains both THC and CBD, is in the form of a mouth spray. However, although this medicine is used in Canada and Europe to provide pain relief for people with cancer and both pain and spasticity for people with multiple sclerosis (MS), it is not yet available in the United States. As of August 2014 the drug was in the final phase of clinical trials required for FDA approval.

A special strain of medical marijuana, named Charlotte's Web for Charlotte Figi (pictured with her dad), grows inside this Colorado greenhouse. Charlotte has a rare and severe form of epilepsy known as Dravet syndrome. Treatment with medical marijuana has given her the chance of a normal life.

Lung Problems

Because other countries are successfully using marijuana to treat medical conditions, some people say there is no question that marijuana should be made legal for all medical purposes in the United

Pregnancy Dangers

Research has failed to show a correlation between using marijuana during pregnancy and delivering a child with birth defects. However, this does not mean that it is safe for a woman to use marijuana during pregnancy. Smoking marijuana while pregnant is associated with a lower birth weight and later problems with the child's memory. Studies also suggest that children whose mothers used marijuana while pregnant have a higher incidence of attention deficit disorder, learning disorders, aggression, and depression; and physicians have noted that some newborns exhibit signs of marijuana withdrawal after birth. In addition, experts point out that smoking marijuana carries a risk that pesticides will be ingested along with the smoke if the substance has not been adequately tested for quality, and this could harm the fetus as well. There is also a potential risk to the mother, since women who smoke marijuana throughout their pregnancies exhibit a higher risk for pregnancy and delivery complications.

States. But opponents to legalization counter that the United States has strict drug standards for a reason: to ensure that a medicine is not rushed into use without first understanding all of the repercussions of its use—and some effects of marijuana use could cause concern. As CNN reporter Jacque Wilson notes: "It's a bit like the fairytale, 'Jack and the Beanstalk.' This 'magic' plant that could help with everything from glaucoma to Lou Gehrig's disease could also contain unknown dangers to our heart, lungs and brain."[26]

For many years people have been concerned that smoking marijuana might cause lung cancer just as smoking tobacco does. However, a study reported in 2013 suggests that such concerns have been unfounded. A team of investigators from Canada, New Zealand, Great Britain, and the United States examined cases throughout the world and determined that people who smoke marijuana, whether occasionally or regularly, have no more risk of developing lung cancer than people who do not smoke it. Another review of cases, led by pulmonologist Donald P. Tashkin of the Pulmonary Function Laboratory at the David Geffen School of Medicine at the University of California, Los Angeles, found that the risk of developing lung problems is far less for marijuana smokers than for tobacco smokers.

Heart Attacks

In regard to the heart, however, studies suggest there is some cause for concern. Smoking marijuana can increase a person's heart rate for up to three hours and can also produce swings in blood pressure. Since high blood pressure can be a warning sign of an impending heart attack—because it means that the heart is pumping blood into blood vessels with too much force—some experts believe that smoking marijuana increases the risk of a heart attack, and research appears to bear this out.

In one study in France, reported in 2014, researchers examined cases of marijuana abuse that occurred between 2006 and 2010 and found thirty-five people who experienced a heart problem. Twenty had a heart attack and nine, or 25 percent, died of heart disease. Moreover, during the period studied the percentage of heart disease among marijuana abusers more than tripled, from 1.1 percent to 3.6 percent.

Since France has roughly 1.2 million recreational marijuana users, critics of the study note that this is an extremely small number of marijuana-related heart problems—if indeed they are related to marijuana, since many of the individuals had other risk factors for heart disease such as high cholesterol. However, some physicians in the United States do find the results of the study concerning, particularly since they fit with some of the heart patients they themselves have seen. For example, cardiologist Valentin Fuster of Mount Sinai Heart Institute in New York City says: "I am concerned about cannabis because we are running a clinic of young people who come to us with coronary artery disease, and I have seen a number of cases in whom I was not able to identify any other risk than the use of cannabis. . . . I am not sure if cannabis is more risky than cigarette smoking or less, but one thing is clear: it is affecting young people."[27]

Robert Eckel, cardiologist at the University of Colorado Anschutz Medical Campus in Aurora, Colorado, agrees. He also points out that since not everyone who has a heart attack is willing to report having used marijuana in the hours before the event, it is unclear just how widespread the problem might be. He says: "Ultimately less than 5% of cases involving drugs of abuse are reported. So let's say we're only reporting one out of 25 to one out of 30 cases. This could be really a substantial problem."[28]

Mental Problems

There is also evidence that marijuana can cause mental problems. Research suggests that people ages eighteen to twenty-five who use the substance regularly can experience some cognitive problems and a decline in IQ points. In addition, studies have shown that very high doses of marijuana can cause hallucinations and/or paranoia, and long-term use at high levels can cause psychosis, a severe mental disorder involving a loss of touch with reality. Marijuana can also aggravate existing mental health problems. In fact, according to the National Alliance on Mental Illness (NAMI):

> The overwhelming consensus from mental health professionals is that marijuana is not helpful—and potentially dangerous—for people with mental illness. Using marijuana can directly worsen symptoms of anxiety, depression or schizophrenia through its actions on the brain. People who smoke marijuana are also less likely to actively participate in their treatment—missing more appointments and having more difficulty with medication-adherence—than people who abstain from using this drug.[29]

However, it is difficult to tell how an individual user will be affected by cannabis because its effects depend on how it is grown, how its active materials are extracted from the plant, the potency of a particular batch, and how it is consumed. John Oram, cofounder of CW Analytical, a scientific lab that tests medical marijuana for quality, says that while the majority is safe, roughly 10 percent can be considered dangerous, although to what degree can be impossible to tell until after the damage has been done. Some may be unsafe because of potency problems (too much or too little THC) or possible contamination by substances such as bacteria, mold, yeast, and pesticides.

Self-Medicating

Even more unsafe, critics of legalization say, is the fact that people who smoke medical marijuana in their own homes control their own dosage and probably do not know the potency of what they are smoking at any given time. This is different from taking a pill that delivers a consistent dose of medication. Some physicians find the lack of dosage control with smoking marijuana so worrisome that they will not prescribe cannabis unless it is to be administered as a pill or tincture in a clinical setting.

Physician Ogechi "Helen" Mbakwe of the Central Washington Internal Medicine and Endocrine Center in Yakima, Washington, argues that there is another reason not to prescribe medical marijuana. She believes that the substance's ability to reduce pain eliminates an important warning system that lets patients and their physicians know when a medical problem is getting worse. She explains: "If we mask these [symptoms] by giving them marijuana and giving them euphoria, the disease progression will keep getting worse and things like organ damage and severe problems will still occur."[30]

Others, however, counter that there are ways to monitor a patient's health that do not require the patient to remain in pain. They also point out that if someone with significant pain is not using marijuana to manage that pain, then this sufferer is most likely using some other prescription pain medication. Many of these drugs, such as oxycodone, can be highly addictive and have serious side effects. Indeed, even those opposed to medical marijuana legalization say that more concern should be paid to these other drugs, particularly because studies have shown that in the United States alone over 15 million people abuse them.

Experts continue to disagree on whether marijuana use should also be a matter of great concern. Some say that regardless of whether the substance offers medical benefits it has at least

"The overwhelming consensus from mental health professionals is that marijuana is not helpful—and potentially dangerous—for people with mental illness."[29]

—National Alliance on Mental Illness.

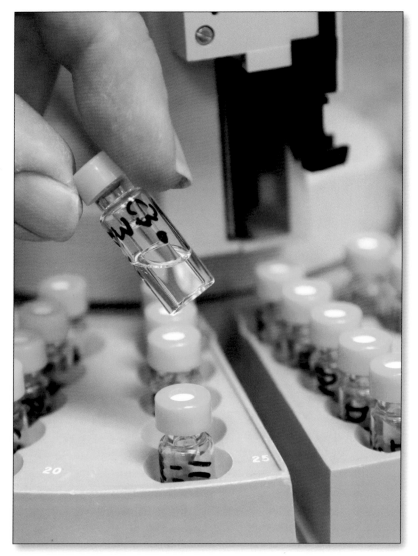

A lab technician prepares vials of medical marijuana for testing, which is required in some states. The effects of medical marijuana depend on variables such as how it is grown, potency of a particular batch, and how it is consumed.

proven itself to be relatively harmless, given how many people have used the drug with no apparent ill effects. Others, however, counter that as the number of users grow there could be a corresponding growth in the problems that scientists suspect might be linked to marijuana use, such as an increased risk of having a heart attack. Moreover, given the dearth of long-term studies it is difficult to determine exactly what the consequences of consuming marijuana over many years might be. Consequently both pro- and anti-marijuana groups have called for more research into the drug's effects.

Facts

• Voters in Colorado legalized marijuana in the year 2000.

• In Washington State the possession of medical marijuana became legal in 1998, but it could not be bought or sold, only grown for personal use.

• According to a 2014 article in the *New England Journal of Medicine*, emergency room visits associated with marijuana use increased by nearly thirty thousand between 2004 and 2011.

• Although the FDA has not approved marijuana, it has approved two drugs made with cannabinoids, xdronabinol and nabilone, to treat chemotherapy-related nausea and vomiting in patients who cannot be helped by other medicines.

• A poll released by the Pew Research Center in April 2014 shows that more than 60 percent of Americans believe alcohol is more harmful than marijuana to individuals' health and to society.

• In 2013 Maine and Oregon added post-traumatic stress disorder (PTSD) to the list of conditions that qualify someone to receive a prescription for medical marijuana, based on new research that suggests the substance is helpful in treating this condition.

CHAPTER THREE

How Would Legalization of Recreational Marijuana Affect Society?

Debates surrounding the legalization of marijuana typically distinguish between two types of marijuana use, medical and recreational, because each has a different impact on society. Legalizing medical marijuana involves allowing people to obtain the drug after a physician has authorized its use, much as occurs with prescription drugs that are already legal. Legalizing recreational marijuana requires the establishment of a new legal, regulated marijuana market, similar to the one for alcohol, for individuals who simply want to enjoy the mood-altering effects of marijuana.

The idea of making marijuana as easily available as alcohol makes some people uncomfortable. According to a March 2014 poll by National Public Radio (NPR) and Truven Health Analytics, although 78 percent of Americans support legalizing marijuana for medical purposes, only 43 percent support legalizing it for recreational purposes. However, polls also show that young people are more open to the idea of legalizing recreational marijuana than are older people. In a survey of Connecticut voters released in

May 2014, for example, 80 percent of people between eighteen and twenty-nine years of age were in favor of making recreational marijuana legal, while only 34 percent of those over age sixty-five favored this.

These statistics lead some experts to believe that over time there will be a stronger and stronger push to make recreational marijuana legal throughout the United States. As Kelly Alexander, a North Carolina representative who is trying to get a constitutional amendment passed in his state to legalize both medical and recreational marijuana, says: "It's an inevitable thing. Trying to stop that movement reminds me of somebody marching out to the beach, holding up their hand and saying the tide will not rise."[31]

Opponents of legalization, however, believe that as recreational marijuana becomes established in a few states, problems will occur that will convince people that the tide needs to be turned. These problems, critics say, have not yet had time to become evident because it was only in 2014 that Colorado and Washington became the first states to provide a state-legal way for anyone age twenty-one or older to buy marijuana for recreational purposes.

Crime Concerns

Nonetheless, many people have speculated on what the problems with recreational marijuana will be. For example, shortly after Colorado and Washington voters decided to make the drug legal for recreational purposes, law enforcement officials warned that it would cause all types of crimes to increase. The sheriff of Colorado's Douglas County, David Weaver, said: "Expect more crime, more kids using marijuana and pot for sale everywhere. I think our entire state will pay the price."[32]

However, in July 2014, after six months of recreational marijuana sales in Colorado, statistics showed that the city of Denver actually had a reduction in crime. Violent crime—including homicide, robbery, and sexual assault—was down 3 percent from the same period in 2013, and the numbers of robbery and burglary cases were the lowest they had been in three years. Property crime overall was down more than 11 percent. In addition, an undercover

> "Expect more crime, more kids using marijuana and pot for sale everywhere. I think our entire state will pay the price."[32]
>
> — Sheriff David Weaver, Douglas County, Colorado.

A long line forms to buy recreational marijuana in Colorado in January 2014. A study later in the year found that almost half of those buying recreational marijuana in Colorado were from other states.

police sting operation that involved sending underage customers into twenty different recreational marijuana dispensaries showed that sellers are careful to check IDs. (Although *dispensary* generally refers to a place that provides medicines, many people now use the word to refer to both recreational and medical marijuana stores.) Not one minor in the sting was able to buy the drug.

A nationwide study from the University of Texas at Dallas released in March 2014 supports the idea that marijuana legalization can reduce crime. This study examined crime rates across the United States in regard to homicide, rape, robbery, assault, burglary, larceny, and auto theft between 1990 and 2006—a period when eleven states (Alaska, California, Colorado, Hawaii, Maine, Montana, Nevada, Oregon, Rhode Island, Vermont, and Washington) legalized medical marijuana. None of these crimes increased in states that had legalized medical marijuana. Moreover, homicide and assault decreased in states where medical marijuana was legalized. Although this decrease might not have been due to the legalization of marijuana, the statistic still shows that marijuana availability did not have a measurable impact on violent crime.

Taking Marijuana Out of Colorado

However, one type of crime does appear to have increased as a result of marijuana legalization: Drug dealers are buying large quantities of marijuana in Colorado for sale in nearby states where the substance is illegal. According to the DEA, Kansas has been hit particularly hard by this problem. In April 2014 Michele M. Leonhart reported that the state saw a 61 percent increase in seizures of marijuana that had come into Kansas from Colorado.

Moreover, a study released in July 2014 found that nearly half of all recreational marijuana purchases in Colorado were made by out-of-state visitors, most of whom planned to take the substance home with them even though transporting marijuana across state lines is illegal under federal law. Experts who study illegal drug trafficking say that Colorado's recreational marijuana has ended up in forty different states. In addition, federal officials estimate that they are apprehending only 10 percent of the people who are driving marijuana across Colorado's borders.

However, Brian Vicente, executive director of the pro-legalization organization Sensible Colorado, says that concerns about this problem are overblown. He says: "Law enforcement has been overly worried about marijuana for 80 years. Law enforcement can point to [only] a couple dozen incidents of people shipping marijuana outside of the state in the 12 years we've had medical marijuana."[33] Vicente also argues that as Colorado's marijuana market and its safeguards become more firmly established, law-abiding citizens will become more aware of the state's marijuana regulations and this will prevent abuses. That will enable police to focus their efforts on catching hardened criminals who seek to sell not only marijuana but also other drugs illegally on the black market.

"Law enforcement has been overly worried about marijuana for 80 years."[33]

— Brian Vicente, executive director of the pro-legalization organization Sensible Colorado.

Gateway Drug

But some critics say that crime is not the primary issue when it comes to making marijuana as accessible as alcohol. They argue that the social ills that will come with this type of nationwide legalization are far more serious. For example, in March 2013 former DEA administrator Peter Bensinger said, "There is a bigger danger

Brain Changes?

In April 2014 a study at Northwestern University found that the brains of marijuana users appear to be physically different from the brains of nonusers. This study used functional magnetic resonance imaging (fMRI), which measures brain activity by detecting changes in blood flow within the brain, to compare the brains of twenty college students who occasionally smoked marijuana with those who never smoked it. The brains of marijuana users differed in terms of volume, density, and shape in parts of the brain associated with emotions, motivations, and certain types of mental illness. This has led people to conclude that marijuana use might be capable of damaging the brain.

Critics of the study, though, point out that the differences noted by the researchers cannot be called damage, since only mentally and physically healthy individuals were allowed to participate in the study. That is, the marijuana users came to their fMRI sessions just as mentally fit as the nonusers. The study was also incapable of determining whether the marijuana use actually caused the observed differences. Perhaps the brains of the marijuana users had been changed by their exposure to marijuana—but it is also possible that people with such brains are naturally drawn to use mood-altering substances like marijuana.

that touches every one of us. In states that have legalized medical marijuana, drug driving arrests, accidents, and drug overdose deaths have skyrocketed. Drug treatment admissions are up and the number of teens using this gateway drug is up dramatically."[34]

By "gateway drug," Bensinger is referring to the theory that using marijuana can lead someone to want to try other, more dangerous drugs such as heroin and cocaine. However, statistics do not bear out this theory, since millions more people have tried marijuana than have tried heroin or cocaine. In fact, according to the federal government's 2012 National Survey on Drug Use and Health, which asked people about substance use within the past month, there were 18.9 million marijuana users compared to 1.6 million cocaine users and 669,000 heroin users.

But while the drug itself may not influence users to take other kinds of drugs, criminals might. The Marijuana Policy Project, an organization working for marijuana policy reform in the United States, says that many experts believe "it is marijuana's illegal status that is the real gateway."[35] The group explains that this is because a person seeking marijuana in a state where there is no legal way to obtain it will turn to drug dealers, and these criminals are likely to encourage the marijuana user to try other drugs—typically ones so addictive that the user will become a steady customer.

"It is marijuana's illegal status that is the real gateway."[35]

— Marijuana Policy Project.

Addiction

Experts disagree on just how serious the problem of marijuana addiction is. Studies indicate that only 9 percent of people who begin using marijuana when they are over the age of eighteen will become addicted to the substance. To some people, this is a small number, given that a 2013 Gallup poll found that one-third of American adults—or roughly 80 million people—have tried marijuana and, according to the National Survey on Drug Use and Health, in 2013 almost 20 million Americans used marijuana regularly.

However, the National Survey on Drug Use and Health also determined that in 2012 2.7 million people over age twelve could be considered addicted to marijuana—hardly an insignificant number. Moreover, for users who began consuming marijuana when they were younger than eighteen the risk of addiction doubles, as can also be the case for people who use cannabis daily. Therefore although it is difficult to predict exactly which users will become addicted, smoking marijuana does pose a genuine risk of addiction, and many users are not aware of this danger.

In addition, as Bensinger noted, marijuana-related accidental overdoses and treatment admissions have increased since medical marijuana began to be legalized. The DEA's 2013 National Drug Threat Assessment Summary reports that there was a 59 percent increase in marijuana-related visits to the emergency room between

2006 and 2010. In addition, marijuana-related treatment admissions during this period rose 14 percent.

But here again, marijuana legalization supporters point out that the total number of marijuana users in America must be considered. As *Washington Post* reporter Christopher Ingraham notes: "When you consider that there are approximately 70 times more marijuana users than heroin users in the United States, it makes sense that more of the former are going to the hospital than the latter."[36] But with so many users, even a relatively small number of cases can still stretch medical resources in a community.

Marijuana Poisoning

Of those who seek emergency treatment related to marijuana use, some are suffering from withdrawal symptoms. Occurring within a week of an addict quitting marijuana, these symptoms can include mood changes—most likely depression, anxiety, irritability, insomnia, and mild intestinal problems, or a combination thereof. However, the symptoms of marijuana withdrawal are relatively minor and short-lived compared to those for other addictive substances, and only about one-half of marijuana users experience any symptoms at all.

Another reason people seek medical help related to their marijuana use is that they feel ill after consuming too much of the substance for their tolerance level, a condition commonly known among users as "greening out." However, experts say that it is impossible for someone to overdose on the drug—that is, to use so much of it at a time that it can be fatal. In a 1998 finding of fact, DEA administrative judge Francis Young noted that for marijuana to kill someone, that person would have to smoke nearly fifteen hundred pounds of marijuana within about fifteen minutes.

But while people cannot overdose on marijuana, some individuals can get an extreme form of greening out, or marijuana poisoning, from consuming too much of it at a time. The symptoms of marijuana poisoning are dilated pupils, nausea and vomiting, problems breathing, extreme feelings of paranoia, and the desire to lie down immediately. In children who develop marijuana poisoning, usually from consuming foods such as brownies with marijuana as an ingredient, these symptoms can be severe, but the child still typically recovers completely within a day or two. The treatment for marijuana poisoning is simply to make the patient comfortable until the marijuana leaves the system.

Conflict with Alcohol

Experts believe that illness is more likely to happen if a person drinks alcohol and then smokes marijuana. The reverse—smoking marijuana and then consuming alcohol—does not appear to make people sick. Experts say this is probably because alcohol in a person's system can cause the body to absorb the THC in the marijuana much more rapidly.

Health experts note that widespread legalization of recreational marijuana will likely increase the chances that people will experience greening out as well as some of the other adverse effects of combining alcohol and marijuana. Since alcohol and marijuana are both depressants, when they are consumed in combination the marijuana can intensify the depressant effects of the alcohol and vice versa, making a person feel more drunk or stoned than would be expected given the amount of alcohol and marijuana consumed.

In addition, someone who has combined marijuana and alcohol can feel the extreme paranoia and other symptoms common with marijuana poisoning, or they might have the extreme vomiting of someone with alcohol poisoning. On the other hand, since marijuana inhibits vomiting, a person who is drunk might not be able to throw up the alcohol. This can result in alcohol poisoning. It can also increase the risk of an intoxicated person choking on his or her own vomit.

Drugged Driving

Because marijuana can magnify the effects of alcohol, many people are concerned that legalizing recreational marijuana will increase the number of accidents attributable to drunk driving. A similar concern is that it will increase the amount of drugged driving. This occurs when someone drives while under the influence of a drug, prescription or illegal, to the point where he or she is dangerously impaired.

Studies have shown that any measurable amount of THC in the bloodstream means that the risk of the driver getting in an accident will be double that of when he or she is sober. Yet it is extremely difficult for a police officer doing a roadside traffic stop to determine whether a driver is under the influence of marijuana. The conventional test for impairment is a roadside coordination test that includes having the driver walk heel-to-toe and then stand on one foot. Studies have shown that 88 percent of drunk drivers fail this test—but only 30 percent of people under the influence of THC do. This number rises to 50 percent for people who have only just started using marijuana, probably because their bodies have not had time to develop a tolerance for the drug.

Consequently police in Colorado have been receiving special training in how to recognize subtle signs of drugged driving. In addition, experts in drugged driving are pushing for the adoption of a handheld device used by officers in Europe to determine marijuana impairment. This device allows police to swab drivers' mouths to test their saliva during a traffic stop, which shows whether marijuana has been consumed within the last four hours.

Testing Methods

Currently, though, US officers must use a urine or blood test to determine the presence of THC in a suspect's body. These cannot be administered during a roadside stop; they must be administered after arrest, and results are not available for days. Most states rely solely on a urine test to determine guilt, even though a positive result on such a test does not prove that the driver was under the influence at the time of the arrest. This is because the active chemicals of marijuana remain in the body for so long that someone who has given up marijuana after smoking it regularly for months can still test positive for the drug thirty to ninety days after quitting the habit.

In legalizing recreational marijuana, Colorado addressed this problem by making a blood test the standard way to determine whether someone suspected of drugged driving is actually guilty of this crime. Instead of providing a positive or negative result, this test measures the exact amount of THC in the bloodstream, and anyone whose level of active THC is more than 5 nanograms (ng) per milliliter of blood is considered guilty. This amount of THC was chosen because it is high enough to prevent someone who has not smoked marijuana for a day or more before driving from being found guilty. Unfortunately, for a few marijuana users the level drops below 5 ng just three hours after the consumption of

marijuana, which means they could be considered not guilty even though they were actually driving impaired.

Because the first major study on this issue is still ongoing, just how stoned is too stoned to drive remains unclear. In July 2014 *USA Today* reported that federal scientists had spent the past year trying to determine an acceptable level of drug influence. Using a driving simulator, the scientists evaluated individuals' driving skills during a forty-minute simulated road test after the driver had consumed marijuana, or some combination of marijuana and alcohol, or a placebo. However, the scientists say it will take them a while to evaluate their data and come up with an idea of just how various levels of these substances affect driving.

A Colorado state trooper trains in testing marijuana-impaired drivers during a simulated roadside stop. He uses a flashlight and a device that measures the pupils of the eyes in an effort to determine the level of drug impairment.

Transporting Marijuana

Given the complexities of determining whether a driver is truly impaired by marijuana while behind the wheel, it is difficult to know just how serious the problem of marijuana-related drugged driving is. Some studies suggest that marijuana use is connected to

Effect on Creativity

Few studies have been done on the effect of marijuana on creativity. One such study reported in 2012, however, suggests that the substance does improve creative thinking. Conducted at the Clinical Psychopharmacology Unit of University College London, this study tested 160 marijuana users both while they were sober and while they were under the influence of cannabis and discovered that those who were "low creatives" became "high creatives" when stoned, particularly in regard to verbal fluency. But a study in 2011 at Texas A&M University found that when creative problem-solving skills were tested after people had consumed alcohol or marijuana, their creativity improved based on their expectation that it would improve. That is, people who believed before the test that alcohol or marijuana would make them more creative actually became more creative. Those who did not believe that a substance would enhance their creativity were no better at creative problem-solving while under the influence of alcohol or marijuana than when they were sober.

25 percent of drugged driving cases, and a 2012 government survey on drug-related behaviors found that 10.3 million Americans admitted to having driven while under the influence of an illegal drug, though not necessarily marijuana. However, other 2012 surveys suggest that marijuana is most often consumed at home, which would suggest that far fewer people are driving while under its influence than, for example, someone who uses alcohol, which is often consumed at bars, restaurants, and parties.

But opponents to legalizing recreational marijuana suggest that residents of states where marijuana is illegal who travel to another state in order to purchase the substance might be tempted to consume some on the way home. Anecdotal evidence seems to bear this out. Police officers in states that border Colorado report that they have been making more arrests for drugged driving that involve marijuana now that Colorado has begun selling recreational marijuana. For example, in Chappell, Nebraska, only thirty drivers were arrested on felony marijuana charges in the area in 2013, but between January and June 2014 there were thirty-two such arrests.

Public Acceptance

Another concern of those opposed to recreational marijuana legalization is the question of how it will affect young people. Parents fear that as recreational marijuana use spreads, children will be increasingly likely to gain access to it, if not at dispensaries then at home. And even if children do not have personal contact with cannabis, some say, they will at least become curious about the substance and see nothing wrong with using it.

Some go even further with their concerns for America's children if recreational marijuana is allowed to remain legal in Colorado and Washington and then spreads elsewhere. They say that the United States will have the same problems as the Netherlands, where marijuana is technically illegal but the police cannot prosecute anyone simply for having a small amount. In the city of Amsterdam, teenagers have felt so free to use the drug that some were coming to class stoned, and educators demanded that the government take action to combat this trend. In response, in December 2012 the city banned smoking marijuana on or near school grounds.

Townhall.com columnist Andrew Tallman suggests that this type of problem should have been easy to foresee, given the behaviors that have stemmed from the legalization of alcohol. He says that our history with alcohol teaches us that if the United States legalizes recreational marijuana then "there will be more use of it than there is currently, which means more young users, more occasional users, more regular users, and more impaired driving. Needless to say, none of this will make our country stronger."[37]

Indeed, some warn that the United States is already being weakened by recreational marijuana because of signs that it is on its way to being acceptable in American society. James L. Capra, the chief of operations at the DEA, complained in January 2014: "There are more dispensaries in Denver than there are Starbucks. The idea somehow people in our country have that this is somehow good for us as a nation is wrong. It's a bad thing."[38]

But proponents of marijuana legalization point out that unlike coffee—which can contain caffeine, another addictive substance—recreational marijuana cannot be consumed in public, and this practice will likely never be allowed given the trend to ban smoking tobacco in public. Therefore, they say, the issue of whether to legalize recreational marijuana hinges on whether an individual has the right to consume the substance in private—an act that marijuana proponents believe cannot harm society.

Facts

- Marijuana is the second most common substance (after alcohol) found in the system of a driver who has died in a fatal accident.

- Surveys suggest that nearly 100 million Americans have used marijuana at some time in their lives.

- According to the National Survey on Drug Use and Health, a higher percentage of residents of Rhode Island use marijuana than the residents of any other state, with more than one in eight residents over the age of twelve smoking the substance monthly.

- According to the National Survey on Drug Use and Health, western states have the highest rate of marijuana usage, at about 9 percent, and the South the lowest, at 5.83 percent.

- Experts say that smoked marijuana reaches the brain in only seven seconds.

- The Drug Policy Alliance reports that among people ordered by a court to receive treatment for marijuana addiction, more than a third had not used marijuana for thirty days prior to admission into the treatment program.

- Studies suggest that less than 2 percent of marijuana users age twelve and over seek treatment for marijuana addiction.

CHAPTER FOUR

How Serious Is the Conflict Between Current State and Federal Marijuana Laws?

I n August 2012 a county sheriff visited the home of seventy-year-old Larry Harvey and his fifty-five-year-old wife, Rhonda Firestack-Harvey, to tell them that they were growing more marijuana plants on their property near Kettle Falls, Washington, than was allowed under state law. (Reports vary on the number of plants; they range from sixty-eight to seventy-five.) The plants were not visible to anyone not on the property—except by air, which is how the sheriff knew about them. A pilot flying over the area had spotted the marijuana.

The couple explained to the sheriff that theirs was a cooperative, or co-op, garden, shared by five people with serious medical conditions and prescriptions for marijuana: the two of them, Firestack-Harvey's son and his wife, and a family friend. This group—now known as the Kettle Falls 5—was under the assumption that each of them was allowed to have up to fifteen plants for personal use. However, the sheriff informed them that under

Washington law a co-op garden is limited to a maximum of forty-five plants. He had all but forty-four of the plants removed, lowering the number to one below the limit, but he did not cite or arrest the group. Once the sheriff left, the Harvey family considered the matter at an end.

But the sheriff reported the case to federal authorities, and DEA agents raided the property. They arrested the Kettle Falls 5 and seized not only the plants that remained in the garden but the family car, $700 in cash, five legally owned firearms, and all the marijuana they found in the home. Each member of the group was charged with six felonies: conspiracy to manufacture and distribute marijuana, manufacture of marijuana, possession with intent to distribute marijuana, distribution of marijuana, possession of a firearm in furtherance of a drug trafficking crime, and maintaining drug-involved premises. (According to the family, the guns were used only for personal protection and hunting, since their rural property is in an area with bears, cougars, and coyotes.)

No Excuse

Attorneys for the Kettle Falls 5 have argued that because the group had complied with Washington State law and had valid prescriptions for medical marijuana, the group should not be subject to these charges. Moreover, they had never tried to sell the drug, and the number of plants they were cultivating would not have provided them with enough to sell in any case. In a letter to US Attorney General Eric Holder attempting to persuade him to stop prosecution of the Kettle Falls 5, attorneys for the group write:

> If the immature cannabis plants that were confiscated had actually made it to harvest, the total weight of the dried flowers would have likely limited each patient to a supply of no more than five ounces per month. Considering one to two ounces are needed to make a pound of butter, it's easy to understand how a cookie at night and some tea in the morning could quickly diminish one's supply. The point being, of course, that there would be no cannabis left over to sell or distribute because these patients needed all of it and then some to properly treat their medical conditions.[39]

Nonetheless, in May 2014 a federal judge ruled that this was not a reason to dismiss the charges. What the defendants intended to do with the plants was immaterial. All that matters, the judge said, is that under federal law no marijuana plants can be grown anywhere in the country for any reason.

This ruling means that the Kettle Falls 5 defendants could face a sentence of ten years to life in prison. As of August 2014 they have rejected plea deals, planning instead to fight to change the law. Larry Harvey, attorney for the Kettle Falls 5, says: "It's wrong what the federal government is doing to us. I just want to make sure Congress knows what's happening so they can fix the law and so there's no more money wasted on cases like mine."[40] From the start of the case through May 2014, the DOJ has spent roughly $3 million on the Kettle Falls 5, and experts estimate that it might cost up to $13 million to prosecute all five and send them to prison.

Larry Harvey (left) and Rhonda Firestack-Harvey (center) await the outcome of a case that highlights the disconnect between state and federal marijuana laws. The couple has been growing marijuana in Washington State, where it is legal, but faces federal charges and possible prison sentences.

Mixed Messages

Experts in marijuana-related issues say that the Kettle Falls 5 case underscores the fact that current federal officials are at odds in regard to how to handle the conflict between state and federal marijuana laws. Deputy Attorney General James Cole has said that the federal government will not prosecute people who use medical marijuana, stating: "We're not interested in bothering people who are sick and are using it in the recommendation of a doctor."[41] Similarly, in the official DOJ policy as established in 2009 via a document known as the Ogden memo—written by then Deputy Attorney General David Ogden—federal law enforcement officers and agencies were told not to expend federal resources "on individuals whose actions are in clear and unambiguous compliance with existing state laws providing for the medical use of marijuana."[42] Yet federal agents and prosecutors continue to go after people like the Harveys.

Many people took the Ogden memo to mean that the federal government had decided it was acceptable to dispense and use medical marijuana in a state that had made these actions legal. Consequently people felt more comfortable investing in marijuana businesses, supporting legalization efforts, and being open about their marijuana use—but this escalation of activity was not what the DOJ wanted. Moreover, many DOJ agents felt that the Ogden memo meant simply that they should not go after extremely sick people, but everyone else was fair game.

As a result, federal authorities started raiding dispensaries and arresting anyone involved with marijuana businesses, even tangentially. They also often timed their actions to influence political discussions on the issue. For example, when Montana legislators were debating in 2011 whether to create state-run medical marijuana dispensaries (medical marijuana was already legal in the state), the DOJ conducted widespread raids and high-profile arrests as a way to send the message that the federal government continued to view associating with marijuana as a criminal offense. Consequently, the legislators in Montana who were inclined to support the dispensary law backed away from it.

"We're not interested in bothering people who are sick and are using [medical marijuana] in the recommendation of a doctor."[41]

— Deputy US Attorney General James Cole.

But even as the DOJ continues to pursue people like the Kettle Falls 5, White House officials have said they do not want to interfere with the use of marijuana for medical treatment. Since the passage of Colorado's and Washington's recreational marijuana laws, the administration has also said that it will not interfere with the sale of marijuana in these states providing it is handled responsibly.

The Cole Memo

To underscore this message, in August 2013 Cole sent a memo to all federal prosecutors spelling out exactly what the DOJ's guidelines are in regard to marijuana enforcement. The Cole memo explains that federal resources should be devoted only to certain types of crimes. Specifically, the DOJ's enforcement priorities are to ensure that:

- marijuana is not distributed to minors
- revenue from marijuana sales does not end up in the hands of criminals
- marijuana (in any form) is not diverted from a state where it is legal to a state where it is illegal
- the system that provides state-authorized marijuana is not used to facilitate the trafficking of other illegal drugs or cover up other crimes
- cultivating and distributing marijuana does not involve violence and/or firearms
- drugged driving and other public safety and health problems are prevented
- marijuana is not grown on public lands
- marijuana is not taken onto federal property

The Cole memo then states: "Outside of these enforcement priorities, the federal government has traditionally relied on state and local law enforcement agencies to address marijuana activity through enforcement of their own narcotics laws. For example, the Department of Justice has not historically devoted resources to prosecuting individuals whose conduct is limited to possession of small amounts of marijuana for personal use on private property."[43]

In light of the Cole memo, medical marijuana advocacy groups are understandably upset that the Kettle Falls 5 are being prosecuted for cultivating marijuana on their own property for personal use. Kari Boiter of Americans for Safe Access says: "This case is another glaring example of what's wrong with the federal policy on cannabis. If the Justice Department can continue to aggressively prosecute individual patients without any consequences from the White House, none of these DOJ memos are worth the paper they're printed on."[44]

Federal agents and local authorities raid a medical marijuana growing operation in 2011 in Helena, Montana. The raid was conducted around the time when state legislators were debating whether to create state-run medical marijuana dispensaries.

Aggressive Sentencing

Marijuana advocates say that the Kettle Falls 5 case also shows the lengths to which federal prosecutors will go to punish such defendants. Since the number of plants the group was growing is too small to lead to a lengthy prison sentence, the prosecutors have argued that the Kettle Falls 5 must have had a crop of the same size in previous years to meet their medical needs. By adding the number of plants in these theoretical crops to the number seized at the time of arrest, the US Attorney's office is arguing that the group actually grew more than one hundred plants, a number for which the law mandates a five-year minimum sentence. Since charging the Kettle Falls 5 for using guns as part of their drug activities also comes with a mandatory five-year minimum sentence, this means that if convicted each member of the group will serve at least ten years in prison.

Another case involving aggressive sentencing shows that state and local prosecutors can also be willing to ignore federal guidelines on marijuana enforcement. In April 2014 nineteen-year-old Jacob Lavoro of Round Rock, Texas, was arrested for making a batch of brownies that contained marijuana and hash oil (a concentrated form of marijuana obtained by extracting THC and other cannabinoids from the plant). He was charged with possessing the marijuana and possessing the hash oil, with the latter charge a first-degree felony under Texas law because the oil's THC is concentrated.

However, the amount of THC in Lavoro's batch of brownies was still a relatively small amount, 2.5 grams, which meant that if convicted he might not receive a long sentence even though he was apparently planning to sell the brownies for $25 each. Therefore county prosecutors used a technicality in the law related to hash oil to use the weight of the remaining batter as well as the brownies. Along with 145 additional grams of oil in a jar, this brought the total to over 400 grams of hash, an amount that would bring a mandatory sentence of ten years to life.

Michele M. Leonhart applauds this kind of aggressive sentencing. In fact, she has argued in favor of increasing the marijuana-related crimes for which tough mandatory sentences can be applied. At a Senate Judiciary Committee meeting in April 2014 where she warned of the dangers of legalization, she said: "Having been in law enforcement as an agent for 33 years [and] a Baltimore City police officer before that, I can tell you that for me and for the agents that work at the DEA, mandatory [sentencing] minimums have been very important to our investigations. We depend on those as a way to ensure that the right sentences equate the level of violator we are going after."[45]

High-Profile Arrests

One of the cases often cited as an example of the DEA orchestrating high-profile arrests in order to quash support for pro-marijuana laws is that of popular former University of Montana quarterback Jason Washington. In November 2011 federal agents raided his state-legal marijuana businesses—a growing operation and a medical cannabis dispensary—and his automotive shop. At the time, the medical marijuana industry was thriving in Montana, but after a series of raids in the state that ended with Washington's, the industry started to suffer. Meanwhile Washington was put on trial for making, distributing, and possessing marijuana and for possessing a firearm in furtherance of drug trafficking crime. These crimes could have resulted in a forty-year prison sentence, but after Washington was found guilty in May 2013 he received a sentence of just two years in prison. However, this was substantially more of a punishment than the ones received by his codefendants, who pleaded guilty to conspiring to maintain a drug-related business and were sentenced to either probation or time served. Critics of the DEA's actions note that none of those who got off easy were prominent individuals.

Criticism of DEA

Leonhart has come under criticism for her zeal and rigidity in regard to marijuana enforcement and sentencing. In May 2014 political insiders said that Holder met with her privately to tell her to stop making public comments that were not in keeping with Obama administration statements regarding marijuana policy. Nonetheless, shortly thereafter the DEA put out a policy paper calling the medical marijuana movement a fraud because its leaders' ultimate goal was not really to help sick people. The paper stated: "Organizers did not really concern themselves with marijuana as a medicine—they just saw it as a means to an end, which is the legalization of marijuana for recreational purposes."[46]

The DEA also drew ire from congressional Republicans in 2014 after it ordered US customs officials to seize 250 pounds of hemp seeds that were being transported from Italy to researchers at the University of Kentucky as part of a study into whether the hemp industry could be reestablished in the United States. The plant source of these seeds had been cultivated to be non-psychoactive, which means that no plants resulting from the seeds could stone anyone. Nonetheless, the DEA still deemed them a controlled substance.

In response, Republican senator Mitch McConnell of Kentucky criticized the agency for wasting time and money on something that was not a drug when there were real drug problems in his state, most notably due to an increase in heroin use. The Kentucky Department of Agriculture then sued the federal government to force the seeds' release. The lawsuit was dropped after DEA officials approved a permit allowing the seeds to continue to their destination.

Targeting a Prominent Activist

Many people have also criticized the DEA for targeting Richard Lee, a major backer of a 2010 California proposition that, had it passed, would have legalized possession of up to an ounce of marijuana for people age twenty-one and older who do not have a prescription for the substance. In 2007 Lee had founded an educational facility, Oaksterdam University in Oakland, California, to teach people about cannabis and help them work toward making it legal. Even though the facility was not distributing marijuana, in April 2012 the DEA raided the university, a museum connected to the school, and Lee's home. Agents also raided a medical marijuana dispensary that Lee operated.

"We think this is a campaign by the U.S. attorneys not just to limit but to kill access to medical marijuana in California."[47]

— Stephen Gutwillig, California's director for the Drug Policy Alliance.

In commenting on the dispensary raid, Stephen Gutwillig, California's director for the Drug Policy Alliance, said: "Oakland has one of the most highly regulated systems for distributing medical marijuana in the state. We think this is a campaign by the U.S. attorneys not just to limit but to kill access to medical marijuana in California."[47] But Dale Sky Jones, Oaksterdam's executive chancellor, felt the DEA's actions were more personal. She says: "Clearly, they're trying to knock down one of the leaders in the cannabis reform movement."[48]

Lee himself, however, saw this as something greater. Shortly after the raid he said: "This is one battle of a big war, and there's thousands of battles going on all over. Before he was elected, [Obama] promised to support medical marijuana and not waste federal resources on this. . . . About a year and a half ago, the policy seemed to change. They've been attacking many states, threatening governors of states to prevent them from signing legislation to allow medical marijuana. They've been attacking on many fronts."[49]

Eliminating Arrests

In April 2014 Leonhart stated that her agency was determined to continue fighting marijuana acceptance. A few months earlier James L. Capra, the chief of operations at the DEA, made a comment that led others to think the DEA's approach was due to fear. He explains: "I have to say this . . . going down the path to legalization in this country is reckless and irresponsible. I'm talking about the long term impact of legalization in the United States. It scares us."[50] As a result, many people believe, the DEA is trying to frighten people into backing away from supporting legalization.

But clearly this tactic is not working, since support for legalization continues to grow—along with a lack of support for the DEA. Many Americans oppose the arrest and prosecution of people who have been obeying state laws. In fact, Conor Friedersdorf of *Atlantic* magazine, who visited Boulder, Colorado, in August 2014 to see how the legalization of recreational marijuana was affecting its residents, expresses the common view when he says that he cannot imagine seeing anyone thrown in jail simply for using marijuana. He writes: "As I drove away from Boulder, I wondered what the long-term effects of legalization would be on the people I'd met. . . . One thought I never had was that Boulder would be better off if its marijuana smokers were all imprisoned, or at risk of arrest, or casually breaking the law to facilitate a habit that isn't going away."[51]

Legislative Efforts

Among those who support this position are members of Congress who have introduced bills attempting to curb the DEA's actions.

The two most prominent pieces of legislation in this regard are the Ending Federal Marijuana Prohibition Act and the Respect State Marijuana Act, both put forth in 2013 and both still being discussed in committees as of August 2014. The Respect State Marijuana Act would do as the name implies: force the federal government to respect state laws and leave alone those following the marijuana laws in their state. This would be accomplished by amending the Controlled Substances Act to take away the DEA's power to infringe on states' rights.

The Ending Federal Marijuana Prohibition Act would take marijuana off the federal list of controlled substances and remove it from the purview of the DEA. In April 2014 Holder stated that the Obama administration would be amenable to changing marijuana from a Schedule I controlled substance if Congress authorized such a change. Marijuana issues would then be handled by

University researchers in Kentucky are studying the possibility of reestablishing the US hemp industry, but their work has ignited a federal-state dispute. The hemp seeds (pictured) grow non-psychoactive plants, but federal officials still deem them a controlled substance.

Threatening Doctors

On June 6, 2014, the *Boston Globe* newspaper reported that DEA agents had been visiting the homes and offices of physicians in Massachusetts—where voters made medical marijuana legal in 2012—who were associated with medical marijuana dispensaries and told them that unless they cut all ties with marijuana businesses they would lose their federal licenses to prescribe medications. As one physician told the *Globe* (anonymously, for fear of DEA reprisals), "The gist was to get me to either relinquish the DEA license, if I insisted on continuing with the dispensary, or give the license up 'temporarily' while involved with the dispensary." He added that the DEA agents stressed the fact that if he gave up his license there was no guarantee he would ever get it back. The physician felt he had no choice but to end his association with a medical marijuana dispensary, because otherwise he would have had to close down his medical practice. Other physicians told the *Globe* similar stories, but a DEA representative declined to discuss the issue with the *Globe*.

Quoted in Kay Lazar and Shelley Murphy, "DEA Targets Doctors Linked to Medical Marijuana," *Boston Globe*, June 6, 2014. www.bostonglobe.com.

the same agency that deals with alcohol-related issues; this agency, the Bureau of Alcohol, Tobacco, Firearms and Explosives, would be renamed the Bureau of Alcohol, Tobacco, Marijuana, Firearms and Explosives. The law would also require people profiting from marijuana to obtain a government permit to grow and sell the substance. However, it would also give the states latitude in how to handle legalization at the state level.

Getting Fired

But these laws do nothing to address another problem with the disparity between state and federal marijuana laws. Because the federal government views marijuana use as illegal, federal protections against people with medical conditions getting fired from a job do not apply. That is, under federal law, someone who is using a legal medication cannot be fired simply for using that medication; in fact, people have a right to keep their medical histories private. But prospective and current employees can be subjected to drug tests, providing the company has a stated antidrug policy, and fired if the results are positive for an illegal substance—including marijuana, even if it is legal in their state.

However, this situation might change because of a related legal case. It involves Brandon Coats of Colorado, a quadriplegic who has been using medical marijuana to treat muscle spasms from a severe spinal injury. In 2010 he was fired from his job at Dish Network—which has a zero-tolerance policy in regard to marijuana—after testing positive on a routine marijuana test, even though he was not under the influence of marijuana while on the job. Coats smokes marijuana only at night before bed, to help him sleep. He had worked at Dish for three years without incident.

Coats filed a wrongful termination lawsuit against the company. In 2013 the Colorado Court of Appeals found that the company did have a right to fire Coats. However, the Colorado Supreme Court has agreed to hear arguments on the case in September 2014; if it finds in Coats's favor, the case could end up being heard by the US Supreme Court. Until and unless this happens, though, workers will have to hide their marijuana use and hope their employers will not subject them to a random drug test. In addition, more employers are likely to be sued by employees who have been fired for drug use in a state where marijuana is legal.

Because of the risk of such lawsuits, workplace issues expert Deborah Keary of the Society for Human Resource Management says that businesses should rethink their drug policies—particularly since a positive marijuana test does not necessarily mean an employee has been under the influence while at work. Keary notes: "If you had a martini on Saturday night, or smoked pot on Saturday night, but you're fine on Monday morning, how is Saturday night the employer's business? So I really think they're going to have to change the way they do testing and define impairment."[52]

"If you had a martini on Saturday night, or smoked pot on Saturday night, but you're fine on Monday morning, how is Saturday night the employer's business?"[52]

— Workplace issues expert Deborah Keary, Society for Human Resource Management.

People on both sides of the marijuana legalization issue say that many other changes are needed to adequately address the problems caused by disparities between state and federal laws. The reality is that marijuana is not going to go away, they say, any more than alcohol will. Therefore it is important for state and federal authorities to work together on these problems rather than to injure marijuana users in the cross fire between warring enforcement policies.

Facts

- A poll released by the Pew Research Center in April 2014 shows that 75 percent of Americans believe the sale and use of marijuana will eventually be legal nationwide.

- More than a third of private employers currently have drug-testing policies.

- According to the DOJ, in 2010 the DEA eradicated 10,329,185 marijuana plants, compared to 2,814,903 in 2000.

- The DOJ reports that in 2009 it seized 2,980.74 metric tons of marijuana.

- A federal farm bill enacted in 2014 allows hemp to be grown only as part of research projects authorized by state agricultural departments.

- The Drug Policy Alliance reports that according to FBI crime statistics, in 2012 there was one marijuana-related arrest in the United States every twelve seconds.

- According to FBI crime statistics, in 2012 over 87 percent of marijuana-related arrests were for simple possession.

How Should Marijuana Be Regulated?

A s the first states to legalize recreational marijuana, Colorado and Washington have been called laboratories for testing what works and what does not in regard to regulating the sales of the substance. Ron Kammerzell of the Colorado Department of Revenue, which oversees the state's marijuana industry, says: "You really don't have anything to draw from. You're blazing the trail."[53]

Voters in the two states passed their legalization laws in November 2012; Colorado's first recreational marijuana shops officially opened on January 1, 2014; Washington's on July 8, 2014. But in the two years between passage and enactment, each state had to do a lot of work in order to ensure marijuana sales would be regulated responsibly. Otherwise, advocates feared, the federal government would take action to stop either law from ever being enacted.

Careful Work

Colorado's marijuana law, Amendment 69, charged state legislators with the task of creating a marijuana regulatory system for both recreational and medicinal sales. The governor established a task force consisting of twenty-four individuals associated with various aspects of the marijuana issue, including law enforcement, litigation, consumer protection, health and addiction, and the marijuana industry, to come up with recommendations for its marijuana regulatory system. In contrast, Washington's marijuana law, Initiative 502, charged the three-member Washington State Liquor Control Board with the task of creating its marijuana regulatory system, which was only for recreational marijuana. Medical dispensaries are illegal under state law; marijuana cannot be bought by or sold to patients. Instead they are expected to grow their own marijuana, although with the new law they can purchase it as a customer of recreational marijuana. Both states ended up with clear, well-considered rules and regulations related to recreational marijuana growth, production, and sales.

Many people favored this careful, thorough approach, which was designed to ensure an orderly, controlled market. As Coloradoan Tom Angell of Law Enforcement Against Prohibition said of his state's efforts: "We can show the rest of the nation that when you legalize marijuana, the sky does not fall. That it can be safer and at the same time you can collect more tax money."[54]

Tax Revenue

The amount of marijuana tax money that Colorado collected in the first six months under the new system was $12 million—an impressive amount to some but a disappointment to many. The projected amount was $33 million for the first six months, with an estimated $107 million for the first fiscal year of sales, and lawmakers had already earmarked $27.5 million of this money to build new schools. Now many believe that the first fiscal year of sales will bring in only $30 to $40 million from taxes on the sales of recreational marijuana.

In Washington, where 40 percent of the marijuana tax money is earmarked for the state's general fund and the remainder for drug prevention and treatment programs, it is too early to tell how strong sales will be. However, the state's dispensaries of recreational marijuana, typically referred to as retail dispensaries, did $3.8 million in sales during their first month of operation. Most people consider this a strong start, but they still suspect that the original estimates for the first year of sales—anywhere from $129 million to $450 million—are much too high.

Experts say there are three reasons for the discrepancy between the predicted amounts and the actual amounts. The first is that estimating revenue from a new business is always difficult—so difficult, in fact, that Colorado State representative Dan Pabon says: "If another lawmaker from a different state came to me and said, 'I want legal marijuana sales because of the tax revenue for my state,' I'd certainly make it known for them to take caution. It's not what people expected."[55]

A Shortage of Product

The second reason for less-than-expected retail revenue is that some dispensaries are experiencing a shortage of product. In part this is because of strong demand by customers. It is also a result of the fact that both Washington and Colorado regulate the production of marijuana by requiring growers to apply for licenses. There is a fee associated with applying; and growers, processors, and sellers are subject to marijuana taxes as well.

In Washington this process got off to such a rocky start that by the first day of retail sales, fewer than 100 of the more than 2,600 growers who applied for a license had been approved, largely because only 18 liquor board investigators were reviewing the applications.

A company in Denver, Colorado, that sells edible cannabis displays the state license that authorizes it to operate as a commercial kitchen for medical marijuana. Revenue from taxes and licenses has been lower than expected in both Colorado and Washington.

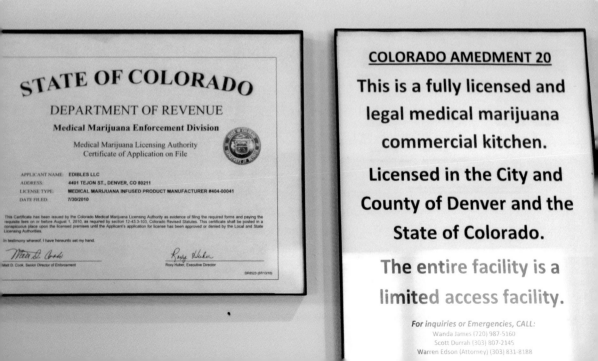

Moreover, only a dozen of those licensed growers had crops ready to harvest. As a result, only 6 of the 25 licensed retail dealers were able to open their dispensaries. A total of 40 retail dispensaries had been licensed by the end of July, but only 18 could offer enough product to be open to customers. Two weeks later, only 16 of them had enough product to sell.

Different Prices

The third reason behind disappointing retail sales is the cost of recreational marijuana as opposed to medical marijuana. In Washington, where medical marijuana is expected to be grown by the patient, there is little cost. In Colorado, there is a fee for the Medical Marijuana Registry identification card required to purchase medical marijuana; obtained via an application process that requires proof that the medication is necessary, its cost as of August 2014 is fifteen dollars. Buyers of medical marijuana must also pay state and local sales taxes on their purchases.

> "If another lawmaker from a different state came to me and said, 'I want legal marijuana sales because of the tax revenue for my state,' I'd certainly make it known for them to take caution. It's not what people expected."[55]
>
> — Colorado State representative Dan Pabon.

Purchases made in a retail dispensary are subject not only to these state and local sales taxes but to additional marijuana taxes as well. For this reason, in Colorado medical marijuana is not sold in the same dispensary as recreational marijuana and vice versa. Colorado retail customers pay a 15 percent excise tax and a 10 percent state marijuana tax; Washington retail customers pay an excise tax of 25 percent. In addition, Colorado cities are allowed to set their local sales tax rate at a higher amount for retail marijuana than for medical marijuana. For example, buyers of medical marijuana in Denver are subject to a 3.62 percent city sales tax, whereas buyers of retail marijuana pay 7.12 percent. Given the other taxes, this means that a buyer of medical marijuana in Denver pays a total sales tax of 7.62 percent whereas a buyer of retail marijuana pays a total sales tax of 21.12 percent. Similarly, on the first day of sales in Seattle, Washington, the city's attorney, Pete Holmes, who was a main proponent of legalizing recreational marijuana, told reporters that of the $80 he had spent on 4 grams of marijuana, $20.57 was for taxes.

An Enterprising Girl Scout

In February 2014 some Californians questioned why there was not a ban on allowing children within a certain distance of a marijuana-related business. This issue was raised in response to news reports that a thirteen-year-old Girl Scout, Danielle Lei, was selling cookies outside a marijuana clinic in San Francisco. Her mother, Carol, was with her and said that Danielle and her sister had sold before in front of places where marijuana is dispensed, but their efforts had not previously attracted media attention. Carol Lei also reported that within just two hours in front of the clinic Danielle had sold 117 boxes. A representative of the Girl Scouts of Northern California said this activity was fine, because the mother was present and the clinic is a legitimate business. However, representatives of the Girl Scouts of Colorado told its members that the organization would not allow its Scouts to sell cookies in that state outside places where marijuana is dispensed.

Skirting the Law

Given the expense of retail marijuana, some people find it unsurprising that more marijuana users in Colorado are buying the substance from medical dispensaries than from retail ones. But experts thought that the opposite would be the case. That is, they assumed that recreational marijuana legalization would result in a reduction in medical marijuana sales, for two reasons. First, retail dispensaries can offer a wider variety of products, and second, medical marijuana users must prove that their health issues warrant a prescription for medical marijuana.

But what many people do not realize is how easy it is to get a prescription for marijuana, not only in Colorado but in other states as well. This is largely because some of the medical conditions that officially qualify a person to obtain a red card are diagnosed through the patient's own report of symptoms. (*Red card* is the common name for the marijuana registry card that shows that the state has deemed someone qualified to purchase medical marijuana.) In Colorado the conditions that rely on a patient's word are migraines, acid reflux disease, and chronic pain. But in California there are dozens of such complaints, including headaches, persistent diarrhea or constipation, impotence, insomnia and other sleep disorders, and chronic writer's cramp.

While interviewing marijuana users in Boulder, Colorado, in August 2014, Conor Friedersdorf came across many healthy people with red cards who were continuing to buy their marijuana at medical rather than retail dispensaries to save money. Some of them knew they were doing something wrong, but others seemed confused about the situation. He reports:

> A few people I met straightforwardly admitted that they gamed the system to get cheaper weed, but many more wanted to do the right thing without being certain what it was. They explained that they're using marijuana for the same reason that other people do yoga, take Xanax or Prozac, or drink a glass of red wine after work. They hesitated when I asked them to categorize their marijuana use; some compared it to paying for a therapeutic massage with their Health Savings Account. One man I met told me he uses weed instead of Ambien [a sleep aid] to reset his circadian rhythm when jet-lagged.[56]

Addressing the Problem

According to the Colorado Department of Public Health and Environment, in 2012 more than eighty-eight thousand Colorado residents had medical marijuana cards. In addition, Friedersdorf reports, Boulder's medical dispensaries serve roughly nine thousand people with red cards. It is impossible to tell just how many of the people with these cards might be healthy. However, experts have determined that so many healthy people are buying at medical dispensaries that the primary customers at retail dispensaries are either tourists or Coloradoans who previously bought marijuana from criminals on the black market.

Now that Colorado legislators are aware of this problem, though, they are going to revisit the issue of how people obtain red cards. Pabon says, "There's some real impact that the medical marijuana market is having on the recreational marijuana market. I think it's worth looking at the taxation on the recreational side but also looking at the rules and regulations on the medical side."[57]

Quantity Controls

Both Colorado and Washington also have controls in place to prevent people from obtaining too much marijuana at once. In Colorado people with a medical ID card are allowed to possess up to two ounces of usable marijuana and up to six marijuana plants, three or fewer being mature ones capable of producing usable marijuana. In Washington people with such a card can possess only an ounce of usable marijuana, but they can also possess sixteen ounces of marijuana-infused product in solid form, seventy-two ounces of marijuana-infused product in liquid form, and seven grams of marijuana concentrate, as well as up to fifteen plants for personal use. Although as the Harveys discovered, there can be no more than forty-five being grown in one communal garden.

In regard to recreational marijuana, both states restrict possession to up to an ounce at a time, although in Colorado someone who does not live in the state can buy only a quarter ounce at a time. But this is not as small an amount as it sounds. An ounce is just over 28 grams, and the average marijuana cigarette contains less than half a gram. In addition, Colorado allows people to grow a small amount for personal use and to give away any surplus. But in Washington all recreational marijuana has to come from a dispensary, and all farmers who provide marijuana to these dispensaries must be licensed.

There are a few other differences in the states' approach to regulating growers. Colorado allows the same person, if licensed, to grow, process, and sell marijuana to consumers, while Washington does not allow a grower and producer to operate a retail dispensary and vice versa. Colorado does not limit the amount of land in the

"A few people I met straightforwardly admitted that they gamed the system to get cheaper weed, but many more wanted to do the right thing without being certain what it was."[56]

— Conor Friedersdorf, staff writer for *The Atlantic*.

Licensed marijuana growers in Colorado and Washington are trying to gauge how much to grow in their states. Too much might encourage people to sell it to minors or in other states; too little might encourage growth of a black market.

state that can be dedicated to licensed growing operations, but Washington does. The state can have only 2 million square feet (roughly 47 acres) devoted to growing marijuana, on the theory that this will prevent so much marijuana being grown that some of it will be illegally diverted to the black market.

Increasing Production

However, given the demand for marijuana in both states, people are calling for an increase in the amount being grown. And as Mike Elliot of the Marijuana Industry Group, a trade association for Colorado's marijuana industry, explains, this is critical to preventing criminals from profiting off marijuana sales. He says, "Basically, the state is trying to ensure that the amount that is being grown in Colorado equals what the demand is. If there is too much, then people want to take it out of state or sell to kids (minors), and if there is too little, then the black market will fill in the gaps."[58]

Indeed, experts in Colorado have determined that as of August 2014 only 60 percent of the marijuana being sold in the state is coming from licensed, legal growers. While some of this illegal growing is being done by otherwise law-abiding citizens, the rest is undoubtedly coming from gang members and other criminals—something that state legislators fear will cause a federal crackdown on the budding industry. They say experts need to stay on top of changing customer needs.

But the ability to do this is complicated by preferences in regard to marijuana consumption. Each method of marijuana use—including smoking; consuming the marijuana as concentrated THC; inhaling a vapor created from heating the cannabis flower, oil, or concentrate; consuming a marijuana-infused edible product; and using a lotion or salve that is absorbed through the skin—requires a different amount of the substance per use, which in turn affects how much of the substance each person will want to purchase. In addition, there are several strains of marijuana, each having a slightly different effect on the user. Different strains are said to be good for different medical problems, and some are more potent than others. The smell and taste that each strain produces varies as well. Edibles, which are produced using not the whole plant but the leaves surrounding the flower, the stems of the plant, the THC crystals that appear on and around the plant, or other secondary products, also have variable effects.

These factors all influence what people want to buy. However, Colorado has devised a way to help dispensaries determine how much of each type of product they will need. Retail vendors record the types and amounts of their sales, and this information is in turn entered into Colorado's State Marijuana Inventory Tracking System. The data in this tracking system, experts believe, will make it easier for marijuana businesses in the future to meet their customer's needs. However, in Washington as of the start of legal sales, no edible makers had yet been licensed in the state.

Limits on Dispensaries

Also to ensure that the public will have enough marijuana to meet its demands, Colorado does not put a limit on the number of licensed dispensaries allowed to operate in the state. However, some cities have banned them, and as of August 2014 only about 200 had been licensed. In contrast, Washington has set a cap of 334 licensed dispensaries statewide, and they must be located in proportion to the population so that there will not be more in an area than the number of customers can support. However, here too, cities are allowed to ban dispensaries from opening in their communities.

Dispensaries are also limited by their cost to operate. Some marijuana business owners say their profit might be too low to make running a dispensary worthwhile, given the taxes involved and the fact that marijuana is cheaper on the black market. Brian Ruden, owner of dispensaries in the Colorado cities of Denver, Colorado Springs, and Louisville, reports: "After the cost of producing each pound, I still have to pay a 15% excise tax, licensing fees, huge rent because landlords overcharge marijuana dispensaries, and when I pay federal income tax I can't deduct like a regular business. I am selling an eighth [of an ounce] for $60 when the street price is about $25."[59]

Ruden cannot deduct his business expenses on his tax return because of the illegality of marijuana at the federal level. For the same reason, it is difficult for marijuana business owners to deal with financial institutions. Although in 2014 the US Treasury Department told banks they could provide a limited amount of services to marijuana businesses without getting into trouble, bankers are still reluctant to get involved with a federally illegal activity. As a result, marijuana businesses are currently cash-only.

Quality Testing

The fact that marijuana is illegal at the federal level also means that the product does not come under the federal laws related to food and drug testing to ensure quality control and safety. However, the marijuana laws in Washington and Colorado do require quality testing. Washington's requirement began the first day of sales, whereas Colorado's requirement was added after sales began.

Marijuana edibles are also subject to packaging laws in Colorado to help ensure that children do not accidentally ingest them.

This law was created shortly after recreational marijuana became legal in the state because hospitals started seeing a rise in the number of children who had eaten something containing marijuana. After this law was enacted in May 2014, its main sponsor, state Senator Mike Johnston, said: "By improving labeling and giving kids a way to tell the difference between a snack and a harmful substance, we can keep kids . . . out of the emergency room."[60]

Colorado law regulates packaging of edible marijuana products (pictured). The law seeks to prevent children from accidentally eating products that contain marijuana and to help adults avoid eating too much too quickly.

Regulating Concentrated Marijuana

Another law was also passed in Colorado to regulate the amount of concentrated marijuana that someone can purchase at any one time. Before this law, an ounce of concentrated marijuana, such as hash oil, was considered the same as an ounce of marijuana in plant form, and there were a number of cases of people suffering from marijuana poisoning.

One well-publicized case involved a college student from Wyoming who was visiting Colorado on spring break. He ingested six times the maximum recommended amount of a marijuana-infused cookie, became violent, and jumped to his death from a balcony. The cookie contained 65 milligrams of THC. Similarly, a prominent *New York Times* columnist, Maureen Dowd, ate significantly more than the maximum dose of a marijuana-laced candy bar while alone in a hotel room, became physically ill and paranoid, and feared that she had died.

Such incidents led Colorado regulators in July 2014 to craft stricter rules in regard to potency and dose size for edibles. State law allows a marijuana edible product to contain up to 100 milligrams of THC. However, under the new law—scheduled to go into effect on November 1, 2014, after a period of public discussion—a product capable of having marked sections, such as a candy bar or cookie that can be broken along scored lines into pieces, can have no more than 10 milligrams in each section, with each section considered a single serving. Edibles that cannot be broken into servings must be packaged so that the contents of each package contain no more than 10 milligrams of THC. In addition, single-serving packages must be child-resistant, and liquid edibles must be in child-resistant containers and clearly marked with information about serving size.

Undoubtedly, more problems will arise as Colorado's and Washington's recreational marijuana markets become established. But so far, each state has demonstrated an ability to address each problem as it arises—and this, say marijuana advocates, will help prevent the federal government from raiding Colorado's and Washington's marijuana dispensaries in the way they have raided those in other states. Mason Tvert of the Yes on 64 campaign, which worked to pass Colorado's marijuana law, says: "I think the federal government has been more respectful of Colorado's marijuana system because it is state and locally regulated. So the federal government has not felt the need to interfere."[61]

However, the existence of these regulations does not ensure that US agents will continue their hands-off approach to the ef-

"By improving labeling and giving kids a way to tell the difference between a snack and a harmful substance, we can keep kids . . . out of the emergency room."[60]

— Colorado senator Mike Johnston.

Unnoticeable Marijuana Use

Some marijuana advocates are concerned that the increasing use of "vape pens"—portable devices that allow relatively unnoticeable consumption of marijuana vapors—will threaten the legalization movement. This is because vape pens make it easy for young people to use marijuana without detection, and the way they deliver cannabis, typically in a concentrated form, makes it up to three times more potent. To address the latter problem, some states that have legalized medical marijuana are considering banning concentrates, and in July 2014 a Michigan court ruled that concentrates are not allowed under that state's medical marijuana law. As for the issue of young people using vape pens, it is unclear how many are engaging in this behavior. However, Emily Anne McDonald, an anthropologist at the University of California at San Francisco, has applied for a grant to study the use of vape pens by young people in Colorado. She has also interviewed teens and young adults in New York regarding their vape pen use and said that the device's popularity is growing, "especially for getting around the rules and smoking marijuana in places that are more public."

Josh Harkinson, "How Vape Pens Could Threaten the Pot Legalization Movement," *Mother Jones*, March 20, 2014. www.motherjones.com.

forts of Colorado and Washington to create a viable marijuana marketing system. Any state that promotes the drug's distribution is still going against federal law, and anyone associated with the marijuana industry can still be federally prosecuted for their actions. This is why those involved in developing marijuana regulatory systems are also attempting to convince the US Congress to pass a law legalizing recreational marijuana nationwide.

Facts

- In Washington, prior to the start of recreational sales, nearly seven thousand people had applied to grow, process, or sell marijuana.

- In 2010 Colorado enacted a law that established a dual licensing system whereby medical marijuana businesses are regulated at both the state and local levels.

- California largely leaves the regulation of medical marijuana up to individual cities.

- As of July 2014 there were 340 medical and recreational dispensaries in the city of Denver, Colorado.

- Among medical cardholders in Colorado, two-thirds are male and one-third are female.

- The potency of some marijuana edibles is ten times stronger than marijuana cigarettes.

- The full effects of a piece (a single dose) of a marijuana cookie might not be felt for an hour or more, which can lead some people to consume additional pieces thinking the amount of THC they originally ate was not enough.

- According to the Colorado Marijuana Enforcement Division, Colorado residents and visitors will ingest or inhale an estimated 287,000 pounds of marijuana in 2014.

Source Notes

Introduction: Harmful or Beneficial?

1. Editorial Board, "Repeal Prohibition, Again," *New York Times*, July 27, 2014. www.nytimes.com.

2. Quoted in Juliet Lapidos, "Readers Respond to the Editorial Series on Marijuana," *New York Times*, July 28, 2014. http://takingnote.blogs.nytimes.com.

3. ONDCP Staff, "Response to *The New York Times* Editorial Board's Call for Federal Marijuana Legalization," *The White House Blog*, Office of the National Drug Control Policy, July 28, 2014. www.whitehouse.gov.

4. Quoted in Lapidos, "Readers Respond to the Editorial Series on Marijuana."

5. John Hawkins, "5 Reasons Marijuana Should Remain Illegal," Townhall.com, January 21, 2014. http://townhall.com.

6. Hawkins, "5 Reasons Marijuana Should Remain Illegal."

Chapter One: What Are the Origins of the Marijuana Legalization Controversy?

7. Quoted in Schaffer Library of Drug Policy, "When and Why Was Marijuana Outlawed?" www.druglibrary.org.

8. Quoted in Peter Guither, "Why Is Marijuana Illegal?," Drug WarRant.com. www.drugwarrant.com.

9. Quoted in Guither, "Why Is Marijuana Illegal?"

10. Quoted in Dale H. Gieringer, "The Origins of California's 1913 Cannibis Law," California NORML, May 2012. www.canorml.org.

11. Quoted in Matt Thompson, "The Mysterious History of 'Marijuana,'" NPR, July 22, 2013. www.npr.org.

12. Quoted in Bob Chessey, "Arts & Culture: Stanley Good and El Paso's 1915 Marihuana Ordinance," *Newspaper Tree*, January 9, 2014. http://newspapertree.com.

13. Quoted in Common Sense for Drug Policy, "The Devil Weed and Harry Anslinger," Public Service Advertisement, Spring 2006. www.csdp.org.

14. Quoted in Ed Rehmus, "Harry J. Anslinger," *Ecphorizer*, no. 83, p. 1249. www.ecphorizer.com.

15. Quoted in California NORML, "The First Pot POW." http://norml.org.

16. Quoted in Schaffer Library of Drug Policy, "History of Marihuana Legislation: Tightening the Law." www.druglibrary.org.

17. Quoted in *New York Times* Editorial Board, "The Federal Marijuana Ban Is Rooted in Myth and Xenophobia," *New York Times*, July 29, 2014. www.nytimes.com.

18. Quoted in Sanjay Gupta, "Why I Changed My Mind on Weed," CNN Health, August 8, 2013. www.cnn.com.

19. *New York Times* Editorial Board, "The Federal Marijuana Ban Is Rooted in Myth and Xenophobia."

20. Quoted in Paul Best, "Support Grows in NC Legislature for Legalizing Marijuana," *Daily Tarheel*, February 10, 2014. www.dailytarheel.com.

Chapter Two: Do People with Illnesses Benefit from Marijuana?

21. Quoted in Medical News Today, "What Is Marijuana? What Is Cannabis?," June 18, 2013. www.medicalnewstoday.com.

22. Quoted in Shaunacy Ferro, "It's Incredibly Difficult to Study Medical Marijuana," Business Insider, August 12, 2013. www.businessinsider.com.

23. Quoted in Ferro, "It's Incredibly Difficult to Study Medical Marijuana."

24. Quoted in Health.com, "Medical Marijuana for Rheumatoid Arthritis?," *Huffington Post*, June 8, 2011. www.huffingtonpost.com.

25. Quoted in Health.com, "Medical Marijuana for Rheumatoid Arthritis?"

26. Jacque Wilson, "Highs and Lows of Using Marijuana," CNN Health, November 12, 2012. www.cnn.com.

27. Quoted in Todd Neale, "CardioBuzz: Is Marijuana Bad for Your Heart?," MedPage Today, April 24, 2014. www.medpage today.com.

28. Quoted in Neale, "CardioBuzz: Is Marijuana Bad for Your Heart?"

29. National Alliance on Mental Illness, "Marijuana and Mental Illness." www.nami.org.

30. Quoted in Health.com, "Medical Marijuana for Rheumatoid Arthritis?"

Chapter Three: How Would Legalization of Recreational Marijuana Affect Society?

31. Quoted in Best, "Support Grows in NC Legislature for Legalizing Marijuana."

32. Quoted in Matt Ferner, "If Legalizing Marijuana Was Supposed to Cause More Crime, It's Not Doing a Very Good Job," *Huffington Post*, July 17, 2014. www.huffingtonpost.com.

33. Quoted in Jace Larson, "Drug Problems Increase After Pot Legalization, Police Say," *9News*, February 5, 2013. http://archive.9news.com.

34. Quoted in Alejandro Acosta, "DEA Chiefs Urge Obama to Nullify Washington and Colorado Laws," RT, March 5, 2013. http://rt.com.

35. Quoted in Marijuana Policy Project, "Is Marijuana a Gateway Drug?" www.mpp.org.

36. Christopher Ingraham, "The Federal Government's Own Statistics Show That Marijuana Is Safer than Alcohol," *Washington Post*, July 31, 2014. www.washingtonpost.com.

37. Andrew Tallman, "Marijuana: No Worse than Alcohol?," Townhall.com, November 2, 2010. http://townhall.com.

38. Quoted in Rick Wilking, "DEA Admits Marijuana Legalization 'Scares Us,'" RT, January 16, 2014. http://rt.com.

Chapter Four: How Serious Is the Conflict Between Current State and Federal Marijuana Laws?

39. Larry Harvey et al., "Letter to Eric Holder," February 26, 2014. https://american-safe-access.s3.amazonaws.com.

40. Quoted in William Breathes, "Washington Family Facing Federal Prison Can't Use State Medical Marijuana Law as a Defense," Toke of the Town, May 7, 2014. www.tokeofthe town.com.

41. Quoted in Mike Riggs, "DEA Responds to Legal Weed in Colorado and Washington: Enforcement of the Controlled Substances Act Remains Unchanged," *Reason.com*, November 7. 2012. www.reason.com.

42. Quoted in Ryan Grim and Ryan J. Reilly, "Obama's Drug War: After Medical Marijuana Mess, Feds Face Big Decision on Pot," *Huffington Post*, January 26, 2013. www.huffington post.com.

43. James M. Cole, "Memorandum for All United States Attorneys," US Department of Justice, August 29, 2013. www .justice.gov.

44. Quoted in Americans for Safe Access, "Five Washington State Medical Marijuana Patients Face Federal Trials," *Daily Chronic*, April 22, 2014. www.thedailychronic.net.

45. Quoted in Phillip Smith, "DEA Chief Opposes Marijuana Legalization, Supports Mandatory Minimums," StoptheDrug War.org, April 30, 2014. www.stopthedrugwar.org.

46. Quoted in Evan Halper, "DEA May Be Losing the War on Marijuana Politics," *Los Angeles Times*, July 12, 2014. www .latimes.com.

47. Quoted in Terry Collins, "Oaksterdam University Raid: Federal Agents Take Over Marijuana College," *Huffington Post*, April 2, 2012. www.huffingtonpost.com.

48. Quoted in Collins, "Oaksterdam University Raid."

49. Quoted in Grim and Reilly, "Obama's Drug War."

50. Quoted in Wilking, "DEA Admits Marijuana Legalization 'Scares Us.'"

51. Conor Friedersdorf, "Life with Legal Weed," *Atlantic*, August 13, 2014. www.theatlantic.com.

52. Quoted in Yuki Noguchi, "Colorado Case Puts Workplace Drug Policies to the Test," GPB News, August 13, 2014. www.gpb.org.

Chapter Five: How Should Marijuana Be Regulated?

53. Quoted in Ana Campoy, "Critics of Legal Pot Say Colorado Isn't Ready Yet," *Wall Street Journal*, December 28, 2013. www.online.wsj.com.

54. Quoted in Josh Harkinson, "Rocky Mountain High," *Mother Jones*, November 7, 2012. www.motherjones.com.

55. Quoted in Kurtis Lee, "In Colorado, Tax Revenue from Recreational Pot Lower than Expected," *Los Angeles Times*, August 12, 2014. www.latimes.com.

56. Friedersdorf, "Life with Legal Weed."

57. Quoted in John Ingold, "Colorado Lawmaker Seeks Marijuana Tax Review amid Disappointing Sales," *Denver Post*, August 12, 2014. www.denverpost.com.

58. Quoted in Katie Kuntz, "Colorado Aims to Produce More Legal Pot," Rocky Mountain PBS I-News, August 13, 2014. www.usatoday.com.

59. Quoted in Kuntz, "Colorado Aims to Produce More Legal Pot."

60. Quoted in Keith Coffman, "Colorado Tightens Control on Marijuana Edibles, Concentrates," Reuters, May 21, 2014. www.reuters.com.

61. Quoted in Harkinson, "Rocky Mountain High."

Related Organizations and Websites

American Medical Association (AMA)
AMA Plaza
330 N. Wabash Ave.
Chicago, IL 60611-5885
phone: (800) 621-8335
website: www.ama-assn.org

The AMA works to improve health care and lower health care costs. To this end, it supports research into health issues and brings physicians together to find ways to better public health.

Americans for Safe Access
1806 Vernon Street NW
Suite 300
Washington, D.C. 20009
phone: (202) 857-4272
e-mail: info@safeaccessnow.org
website: www.safeaccessnow.org

This organization is dedicated to advancing medical marijuana therapeutics and research into the substance's health benefits. Its website provides information on the medical use of cannabis and related legal issues, as well as links to news articles and press information on the subject.

Drug Enforcement Administration (DEA)

8701 Morrissette Dr.
Springfield, VA 22152
phone: (202) 307-1000
website: www.justice.gov

This agency of the federal government is charged with enforcing laws and regulations related to controlled substances. It seeks to reduce and perhaps eliminate access to these substances and to prevent criminals from profiting from them.

Drug Policy Alliance (DPA)

Headquarters
131 W. Thirty-Third St., 15th Floor
New York, NY 10001
phone: (212) 613-8020
e-mail: nyc@drugpolicy.org
website: www.drugpolicy.org

The DPA works to promote sensible drug policies that are grounded in science and to end the war on drugs. Its website provides information on drugs, drug policies, and drug-related laws and rights.

Law Enforcement Against Prohibition (LEAP)

8730 Georgia Ave., Suite 300
Silver Spring, MD 20910
phone: (301) 565-0807
e-mail: info@leap.cc
website: www.leap.cc

An international organization of criminal justice professionals, LEAP is working to end the war on drugs. It educates the public, the media, and policy makers about the failure of current drug policy, which the group feels has led the public to lose respect for law enforcement.

The Marijuana Policy Project

PO Box 77492
Capitol Hill
Washington, DC 20013
phone: (202) 462-5747
e-mail: info@mpp.org
website: www.mpp.org

This organization seeks to increase public support for marijuana policies that do not involve punishing people for their marijuana use. It also works to change state laws so that penalties for marijuana use are reduced or eliminated.

National Cannabis Industry Association

1250 Grant St.
Denver, CO 80203
phone: (888) 683-5650
e-mail: info@thecannabisindustry.org
website: https://thecannabisindustry.org

A national trade association for marijuana businesses, the National Cannabis Industry Association is working toward the establishment of a successful legal cannabis industry in the United States. To this end it defends against threats to the legal market for cannabis and cannabis-related products.

National Institute on Drug Abuse (NIDA)

Office of Science Policy and Communications, Public Information and Liaison Branch
6001 Executive Blvd., Room 5213, MSC 9561
Bethesda, MD 20892-9561
phone: (301) 443-1124
website: www.drugabuse.gov

NIDA supports research into various drugs and helps disseminate the resulting scientific information. It also works to improve prevention and treatment and to improve policies related to drug abuse and addiction.

National Organization for the Reform of Marijuana Laws (NORML)

NORML and the NORML Foundation
1100 H St. NW, Suite 830
Washington, DC 20005
phone: (202) 483-5500
e-mail: norml@norml.org
website: http://norml.org

NORML works to increase public support for marijuana legalization and to ensure that consumers have access to safe, high-quality marijuana. Its website has a wealth of information on marijuana and marijuana-related issues.

The Substance Abuse and Mental Health Services Administration (SAMHSA)

1 Choke Cherry Rd.
Rockville, MD 20857
phone: (877) 726-4727; (800) 487-4889 (TDD)
website: www.samhsa.gov

An agency within the US Department of Health and Human Services, SAMHSA works to reduce the negative impact of substance abuse and mental illness in America. To this end, it has several advisory councils and committees that draw on the wisdom of experts in drug-related issues and mental health.

Additional Reading

Books

Michael Backes, *Cannabis Pharmacy: The Practical Guide to Medical Marijuana.* New York: Black Dog & Leventhal, 2014.

Greg Campbell, *Pot, Inc.: Inside Medical Marijuana, America's Most Outlaw Industry.* New York: Sterling, 2012.

Jonathan P. Caulkins and Angela Hawken, *Marijuana Legalization: What Everyone Needs to Know.* New York: Oxford University Press, 2012.

Doug Fine, *Hemp Bound: Dispatches from the Front Lines of the Next Agricultural Revolution.* White River Junction, VT: Chelsea Green, 2014.

Doug Fine, *Too High to Fail: Cannabis and the New Green Economic Revolution.* New York: Gotham (Penguin Group), 2012.

Peter Hecht, *Weed Land: Inside America's Marijuana Epicenter and How Pot Went Legit.* Berkeley: University of California Press, 2014.

Martin A. Lee, *Smoke Signals: A Social History of Marijuana—Medical, Recreational and Scientific.* New York: Scribner, 2012.

Alyson Martin and Nushin Rashidian, *A New Leaf: The End of Cannabis Prohibition.* New York: New Press, 2014.

David E. Newton, *Marijuana: A Reference Handbook.* Santa Barbara, CA: ABC-CLIO, 2013.

Roger Roffman, *Marijuana Nation: One Man's Chronicle of America Getting High: From Vietnam to Legalization.* New York: Pegasus, 2014.

Internet Sources

Bruce Alan Block—Attorney at Law, "Marijuana Trivia and Facts." http://brucealanblock.com/marijuana_trivia_and_facts.

Bill Briggs, "Puff, Puff, Pink Slip: Legal Weed Use Still Carries Job Risk," NBC News, July 13, 2014. www.nbcnews.com/story line/legal-pot/puff-puff-pink-slip-legal-weed-use-still-carries -job-n153841.

Index

Picture Credits